COUNCIL
PAPERS ON
INTERNATIONAL
AFFAIRS

THE WEST AND THE MIDDLE EAST

BY

JOHN C. CAMPBELL AND HELEN CARUSO

COUNCIL ON FOREIGN RELATIONS, INC.

58 EAST 68th STREET | NEW YORK, NEW YORK 10021

CONTENTS

WE HAVE BEEN ACCUSTOMED to looking at the Middle East as the focus of two long-standing conflicts, one between the Arabs and Israel and the other between the two superpowers. These conflicts are interlocked by virtue of the ties which link the Soviet Union to some of the Arab states (primarily Egypt) and the United States to Israel. We have, accordingly, tended to see the Middle East crisis and its "solution" as a matter primarily for these actors and requiring decisions on their part which will avoid war, reduce the dimensions of conflict, and give promise of greater stability. The views of Britain and France, though given voice in the continuing four-power talks and in public, have not been very much heeded by the four main actors. Other Western nations such as Italy and the Federal Republic of Germany have had very little to say. "Europe," as a group of nations with an obvious interest in peace and stability in the Middle East, has not been heard at all. Nor has Japan.

The Arab-Israel conflict, moreover, is not the only ring in the Middle East circus though it is the one on which the eyes of most spectators are fixed. Another set of problems concerns the maintenance of military commitments, the balance of forces in the Mediterranean and Indian Ocean, and the relationship of force to political competition and to negotiation. These are matters which, in view of the decline of French and British military and political presence in the area, have tended to become almost exclusively the subject of Soviet-American relations. Yet the fate of Greece and Turkey and the growth of Soviet naval power in the Mediterranean are certainly relevant to the security of the countries of Western Europe and to the effectiveness of the North Atlantic Alliance.

A third cluster of problems has to do with oil. In the continued supply of oil from the Middle East and North Africa the stakes of Western Europe and of Japan are far greater than that of the United States. Yet the Western European states, separately or together, have not worked out an effective oil policy, nor have they done so with the United States—except in so far as the positions worked out by international oil companies have represented the views of the home governments of those companies. As for Japan, its government and its oil companies have played a lone hand.

It is apparent from this picture that the advanced noncommunist nations (North America, Western Europe, and Japan) have not clearly defined their interests in the Middle East, or at least that they have not consulted with each other to determine what interests they have in common and might act in concert to protect. Members of the European Economic Community (E.E.C.) have set up procedures to work out a common policy, but they have only just begun to talk about it. Each nation, meanwhile, has tended to follow its own course. France has evolved a Mediterranean policy without reference to global considerations, while Britain has virtually given up its military and political responsibilities east of Suez though hoping to maintain its important economic interests. The United States has attempted to combine a continuing presence and influence in the region with a general inclination to reduce commitments and expenditures on a worldwide basis. The easy identification of "Western" with U.S. interests and policies is no longer standard fare in U.S. policy statements and indeed no longer a reflection of the facts of the situation.

It is, nevertheless, worth asking the question whether present policies are serving the interests of the Western nations and Japan in the best possible way. It is worth examining whether a more prominent role for Western Europe, by itself or in concert with America, would be beneficial to European and to American interests. The first step is to describe as best we can what those interests are, as the respective governments see them. Then we can look at how they may interlock or coincide and, finally, whether common approaches and closer coordination of policies seem called for. This essay considers separately the security question, political interests and the Arab-Israel conflict, and policies relating to oil.

I.

SECURITY: WHAT MILITARY POSTURE?

For twenty-five years the United States and Britain have tried to maintain a defensive position in the Middle East that would hold off the expansion of Soviet power. Right after the Second World War it was largely a British position. The United States took the leading role in Greece and Turkey in 1947 and shortly thereafter in Iran, leaving Great Britain as the leading Western power in most of the Arab world. But the Middle East was not merely an arena for contending great powers. The challenge to British power in the Arab world, in Iran, and in Cyprus came primarily from local nationalism, which the Soviet Union naturally tried to exploit in its own interest. The Suez crisis of 1956 put an end to any meaningful role for the British in the eastern Mediterranean except for their bases on Cyprus and the connection with Malta. In effect, the U.S. Sixth Fleet took the place of Britain's network of treaties, bases, and military dispositions. And the United States thereafter became the main target of radical Arab nationalist movements, whose leaders were disposed to look to Moscow for support.

The British still held their historic positions at Aden and in the Persian Gulf. Nationalist pressures and their own budgetary stringencies in the 1960s then forced them to give up Aden, and in 1968 the Labour government announced that the British military presence east of Suez would be withdrawn by the end of 1971 and that all commitments in the Persian Gulf would be terminated by that time. The coming to power of the Conservative Party in 1970 brought restudy but not basic change in that policy despite pre-election statements that the decision would be reversed. For all practical purposes the United States seemed to have inherited the lion's share of responsibility for defense of the area east of Suez, including the Indian Ocean, without any definite decision to take it up and without military deployments to give it substance. But some fundamental points remained unclear. What kind of responsibility? Defense against what?

By the early 1970s the situation had undergone basic change from that of the 1950s. It was no longer a question of keeping the Soviets out of the Mediterranean–Middle East–Indian Ocean area. They were there. They had established themselves in Egypt, Syria, and elsewhere in the Arab world. Their policy of military aid and diplomatic support to India seemed, with the Indian military victory and the breakup of Pakistan in 1971, to have paid off handsomely in political gains. The question was not how to exclude any Soviet presence but how to adjust to it and keep it short of the capacity to control any critical part of the area or to deny Western access thereto. Would this task, which had both military and political aspects, have to be undertaken by the United States alone? The fact was that no other Western power showed much interest. But how big a task is it? The answer requires an estimate of Soviet policy, a consideration of the interests of other powers which it threatens, and some information on what they are doing about it.

THE SOVIET UNION AND THE MIDDLE EAST

This is not the place either for a history of the advance of Soviet power and influence into the Middle East or for an involved analysis of the motivation behind it. We shall deal with the subject only in rather general and simplified terms, which are roughly the terms in which other governments will look at it in planning their own policies for the future.

Russian policy, in both Tsarist and Soviet forms, has been marked by a push to the south. There it has clashed with the nations on its southern borders, primarily Turkey and Iran, and with the interests of rival powers, most often Great Britain but at times France or Germany, and most recently the United States. Security has lain at the heart of the policy. The need to guard against attack from the south, to prevent potentially hostile powers from establishing positions in states bordering on Russia, to keep in Russian hands the keys to the Black Sea, the Turkish Straits, seemed self-evident in St. Petersburg or Moscow. But defensive is also offensive. Attempts to dismember or dominate Turkey and Iran, to make the doors at the Straits swing outward but not inward, to establish footholds in the Mediterranean and Red Seas, were inevitably judged by Western powers as threats to their imperial lifelines and vital strategic interests.

The southward expansion of Russian power was not constant. It tended to fluctuate according to the balance among the great powers and to the opportunities presented. In the interwar period when the Soviet state was relatively weak and isolated, Stalin was content with a ring of neutral states on its southern borders. In the aftermath of the Second World War he tried to take advantage of easy opportunities that proved not to be there, putting pressure on Greece, Turkey, and

8

Iran and claiming positions in the Mediterranean, only to run up against strong local and Western resistance. He then pulled back and accepted a situation in which the border states joined the Western alliance system. After Stalin, however, new opportunities appeared.

Nikita Khrushchev's diplomatic breakthrough into the Arab world by means of the arms deal with Gamal Abdel Nasser of Egypt in 1955 signalled a new phase of Soviet policy, with two features that have been in evidence ever since. The first was the demonstration that the expansion of Soviet power and influence could not be checked by the territorial barrier of the Western-oriented northern tier consisting of Turkey, Iran, and Pakistan. The other was the acquisition of new positions in the Middle East as part of a strategy that went well beyond the confines of that region. Khrushchev and his colleagues embarked at that time, the middle and late 1950s, on a policy of challenging the Western powers in South Asia, Africa, and other areas of the Third World. That strategy survived setbacks in the Congo, Cuba, and elsewhere, and also survived the fall of Khrushchev. His successors carried it on, with less élan but more attention to the need for military power to sustain it. And while they reduced costs and commitments in some more remote areas, they concentrated all the more heavily on the Middle East.

Egypt, the strongest, most populous and most influential of the Arab states, remained the keystone of the Soviet position. In spite of Nasser's blunders in engaging in a war he could not win in Yemen and in leading his country to a crushing defeat by Israel in 1967, the Soviet-Egyptian tie held firm because both sides needed it. After the six-day war the arms supplies and the political support coming from the Soviet Union became Egypt's only hope of recovering its strength and prestige and, possibly, its lost territory. For the Soviet leaders, Egypt's dependence and the continuing Arab-Israeli tension served as the basis for a military and political position in that country, in Syria, and in lesser degree elsewhere in the Arab world, which went far beyond any previous advance of Russian power and clearly challenged the established positions and interests of the United States.

It is a policy based on the concept of great-power interests despite the ideological language in which it is clothed. The theories and declarations of affinity between the heartland of scientific socialism and the socialist and other progressive forces in the Middle East seem to be necessary for home consumption and for tactical reasons, but they bear little relation to aims and strategy. The Soviet leadership uses the themes of socialism to help gain military and political influence rather than using that influence to spread communism. Seen in that light, Soviet aims and strategy may have a greater flexibility than many outside observers have thought. They are not absolute but relative. The Soviet Union seeks to increase its own power, and therefore its own security, at the expense of the power of its principal rivals, which are now the United States and China.[1] It would like to organize the local states in alignments favorable to itself; if that is not possible, it will try to prevent alignments organized by others. If it can be the primary outside power in the region, the arbiter of local affairs, or the most influential or determining voice in the concert of nations concerned, so much the better. But it is probably a mistake to speak of domination or of communization as an absolute goal animating Soviet policy, for the policy has proved to be flexible enough to allow adaptation of aims to practical possibilities and to the actions of local states and other outside powers. Soviet relations with other communist countries tell something about the difficulties of domination. Thus we need not assume that the push to the south, for all its historic continuity, is not subject to stabilization, deflection, or compromise.

With those points in mind, let us look at the current Soviet military position. As it affects those Middle Eastern countries adjacent to the Soviet Union, it is based on the maintenance of large land and air forces on Soviet territory to which those countries, Turkey and Iran, are vulnerable. This has been so in the past and will be so in the future. The major threat from the north is now supplemented by Soviet naval power to the south, which creates an uneasy sense of encirclement. Turkey and Iran have tried to protect themselves against Soviet attack or pressure by (a) making security arrangements with other powers, and (b) trying to maintain normal and reasonably friendly relations with Moscow. They have succeeded rather well, and Moscow itself has in recent years abandoned threats for gestures of friendship.

Further south, in the Arab world, the Soviets are present with deliveries of arms, with military missions and advisers, and with ships and aircraft making use of local facilities. They are there by invitation of the respective Arab governments. In two cases, Egypt and Iraq, bilateral security treaties exist as a basis, over the next fifteen years, for close military and political cooperation.[2] The Soviet military intrusion is seen as necessary by Egypt and Syria for their own security against Israel, but even these friends and allies do not like it or look forward to its permanence on their own soil. Other radical Arab states such as Libya and Sudan are wary of Soviet influence. Conservative Arab states definitely fear it. And Israel sees the Soviet military presence, especially in Egypt, as a direct threat to its security.

The newer aspect of the Soviet military position is naval power, based primarily in Black Sea ports but also including a permanent Mediterranean squadron varying from some thirty to sixty ships at different times. In addition, since 1968 the Soviet Union has had an occasional naval presence in the Indian Ocean, Red Sea and Persian Gulf through visits of Soviet naval units in those waters, and now an average of ten ships is there at any given time. In the Mediterranean, Soviet ships are able to make use of facilities at Port Said, Alexandria, Mersa Matruh, Latakia and possibly other ports. In the Indian Ocean, Moscow is seeking comparable arrangements. To compensate for the lack of attack carriers (though there are two helicopter carriers), Soviet aircraft have had the use of airfields in Egypt and, at one time, in Algeria also.[3] The Soviet military position is further strengthened by the presence in Egypt of an estimated 10,000 to 15,000 military men as advisers, instructors, and combat personnel. We may assume that the Soviet leaders will attempt to add to these dispositions by increasing the Mediterranean and Indian Ocean naval forces, gaining the use of additional naval and air facilities, and putting more advisers and other military personnel into receptive local countries.

All in all, the Soviets have built up a formidable position of strength. In itself this military strength does not have any great relevance to the question of a major war involving the Soviet Union and the Western powers, although one mission of the force in the eastern Mediterranean is to keep U.S. striking power (carriers and submarines)

1. While China is not a rival of anywhere near equal rank in the Middle East, its activities in the peripheral areas (Yemen, the rim of the Arabian Peninsula, and East Africa) as well as its ties with Pakistan and the interest it has shown in the Palestinian guerrillas make it a factor in Soviet planning.

2. See *Current Digest of the Soviet Press*, Vol. XXIII, No. 21, June 22, 1971, pp. 2–4, and *The New York Times*, April 10, 1972.

3. Jürg Meister, "Risks of Soviet Naval Buildup," *Swiss Review of World Affairs*, November 1971, p. 8; Lawrence L. Whetten, "The Military Consequences of Mediterranean Super Power Parity," *New Middle East*, November 1971, p. 16. The use of Algerian airfields is an obscure point not clarified by published data.

"targeted," and one reason for the presence of Soviet warships in the Indian Ocean is to seek out American submarines armed with Polaris weapons.[4] Its importance lies in its effect on the decisions of others in situations short of major war. One aim is to cause the Sixth Fleet to limit and reduce its operations, preventing such an action as took place in Lebanon in 1958.[5] Others may be by its presence to encourage nations such as Egypt or Syria to be more, or less, belligerent or intransigent as the situation demands; to intimidate other nations; or to offer protection to revolutionary movements. Presumably the Soviet military forces in the region would not interfere physically with the interests of other states in peaceful trade and freedom of access to oil supplies, though their presence might encourage local governments to take such measures.

The function of Soviet military force is thus eminently political. It enables the Kremlin to impress local governments. It keeps before their eyes the reality of Soviet power in contrast to the limited Chinese presence. It enables Moscow to talk on equal terms with Washington on Middle Eastern questions, and to exercise a veto over some Western diplomatic and political endeavors which it does not like. It does not—not yet anyway—put the Middle East in a Soviet sphere of influence.

SECURITY INTERESTS OF THE UNITED STATES

For two decades following the announcement of the Truman Doctrine in March 1947 the United States proceeded on the premise that the Middle East was a vital area in the global balance and that it must be denied to the Soviet Union; that is to say, no part of the area should come under the control or the dominant influence of the U.S.S.R. The reasoning behind the policy underwent changes as conditions changed (e.g., the decline in the need for U.S. bases in the region as part of the global nuclear deterrent to Soviet aggression anywhere), but the policy itself remained. Through cooperation with Great Britain in a common effort to maintain Western positions and through the inclusion of Greece and Turkey in NATO, the United States tried to have the burden of defense of the Middle East shared by Western nations other than itself, but containment was also a national policy which the United States was prepared to support alone if necessary.

During the 1950s the United States took a stand against admitting the U.S.S.R. to the concert of powers which exercised a vague and self-arrogated responsibility for preserving the peace and security of the region. After the Soviet-Egyptian arms deal of 1955 and the Suez crisis of 1956 the U.S.S.R. became in fact a Middle East power, and the others had to take account of it even if they still did not invite the Soviets to sit down with them in conferences to deal with the area's problems. During the 1960s, divergent policies of the Western nations, the shrinking of Britain's role east of Suez, and the emergence of Israel as a significant factor in the regional balance of power have again changed some of the ways in which the United States has played the game, but the general aim remains: to keep the Soviet penetration and presence within tolerable bounds. The policy of the Nixon Administration, for all its emphasis on cutting down commitments to use U.S. forces and on helping others to help themselves, has the same fundamental objective.

One of the perils of the situation is that it is not Soviet and Western military forces alone that make up the local military equilibrium. Those forces on each side are tied to a significant degree into the local balance between Arab and Israeli forces. Thus Abdel Nasser's war of attrition waged with heavy Soviet armament in 1969 brought the extension of Israeli military operations into the Nile valley and the outskirts of Cairo, threatening the Nasser regime and helping to bring on the stationing of Soviet combat personnel in Egypt in 1970. This move, in turn, presented the United States with the question what, if anything, should be done to force their withdrawal. Ultimately Washington decided against any drastic action. After Secretary Rogers's cease-fire and standstill plan was violated by the Egyptians and the Soviets, it chose instead to meet the situation by permitting Israel to purchase large new quantities of American arms. Despite concurrent efforts to promote negotiations for peace, this action, against the background of the Nixon Administration's many statements that it would not allow the balance of power to be tilted against Israel, confirmed that the United States was committed to one side, just as the Soviet Union was committed to the other.

4. Oles M. Smolansky, "Soviet Entry into the Indian Ocean: An Analysis," unpublished paper presented at the Center for Strategic and International Studies, Georgetown University, Conference on the Indian Ocean Area, March 18-19, 1971.

5. Admiral Elmo Zumwalt, Chief of Naval Operations, is strongly of the opinion that the Sixth Fleet is still able to act decisively in such a situation (See *U.S. News and World Report*, September 13, 1971, pp. 72–77).

That situation might bring home to both powers the perils of a local conflict which neither might be able to control, impelling them to seek with each other some arrangement to stabilize the balance and to keep their competition on the political level. In the absence of such an arrangement—and none had materialized by early 1972—each sought to gain political ends while keeping a sharp eye on the military position of the other. The United States was looking not only at the Arab-Israel dispute but also at its commitments to NATO allies in the eastern Mediterranean, Greece and Turkey, at the Soviet threat to nonaligned Yugoslavia, and at the growing Soviet power in the Mediterranean region, which might reach further west across North Africa and threaten the security of Western Europe.

This is a crucial point, the connection between the engagement of Soviet power in the Arab-Israel conflict as a counterpart to that of the United States and the threat of that power to the Western Alliance and the security of its members. To Americans who regarded these two roles as all of a piece, the clear answer was a combined NATO effort to stop the Soviet advance and to protect both Israel and the NATO area; in short, the equivalent of the expansion of NATO to include Israel. Other Americans, however, worried about the extent of commitment to Israel because it alienated Arab leaders and opened up opportunities for a broader and deeper Soviet presence in Arab lands. The Administration did not stress the connection, knowing the reluctance of its European allies to recognize it. Yet they all knew that it existed. They knew that they were threatened with war if the Arab-Israel conflict should again explode, and also that growing Soviet power in the region was bound to have some effect on their own security. Hence the importance of how European states saw the problem.

SECURITY INTERESTS OF OTHER STATES

Great Britain

The British government shares with the United States the aim of denying the Middle East to Soviet domination. It remains concerned over Soviet naval forces (especially submarines) in the Mediterranean and in the Indian Ocean. It still acts as a kind of junior partner to the United States in the Mediterranean, while east of Suez neither seems to want the status of senior partner. Three factors, however, lead Britain to a special view in regard to its own role in a strategy to carry out the common aim. The first is its inability to support a strong military effort. As has been noted above, for all practical purposes its major role in the eastern Mediterranean came to an end in 1956; its presence east of Suez was maintained for another decade, but since 1966 has been cut back to the point where little remained at the beginning of 1972.[6] Britain may have a minor part in multilateral military dispositions in the Indian Ocean and will still make a naval contribution to NATO in the Mediterranean, but the political and budgetary decisions for a low military profile have been made. Second, London has concluded that the particular problem of protecting its own interests in oil, communications, and trade is not suitable for solution by military dispositions but rather by political and economic action. This is partly a matter of necessity, partly a matter of conviction. Hence the emphasis on mutually beneficial relations with Middle Eastern states. Third, the British are skeptical of the theory that the Soviet military buildup will open the way to Soviet control or domination. They seem less alarmed than Americans, perhaps because they know that the major decisions on maintaining deterrence are not their own.

In reaffirming in 1971 Britain's decision to withdraw from the Persian Gulf by the end of the year, Sir Alec Douglas-Home called it "an area of outstanding strategic importance, not only to this country but also to Europe and the rest of the world."[7] But beyond the offer to the putative new Union of Arab Emirates of a treaty of friendship, the existing force of Trucial Oman scouts, British military training teams, and British military exercises and regular naval visits, the backup for this area of outstanding strategic importance would presumably have to be provided by someone else.[8] It need not be a large military commitment. The British knew that the old imperial-type system could never be re-created and did not expect America to step into their shoes. The Persian Gulf states themselves were quick to announce that they needed no foreign protector.

6. *Statement on the Defence Estimates, Part I, The Defence Review,* February 1966 (Cmnd. 2901) and following annual Statements and Supplements through 1971.

7. Statement in the House of Commons, March 1, 1971.

8. It should be noted that neither the Labour statement of 1968 nor the Conservative one of 1971 mentioned any change in the relationship with Oman, which has a British-trained armed force and British facilities at Salalah and on the island of Masirah. Those points are geographically on the Arabian Sea, not in the Gulf.

France

Postwar France has a long history of disagreement with the United States on the question of security in the Middle East and the Mediterranean. After a brief period of U.S.–U.K.–French cooperation based on the Tripartite Declaration of 1950 and the idea of an Allied Middle East Command (1951), France opposed the Baghdad Pact, joined in the attack on Egypt in 1956 for reasons of its own, and withdrew French naval units from NATO's Mediterranean command in 1959. Meanwhile, the process of decolonization in French North Africa was studded with French-American controversies until Algeria finally won its independence in 1962.

Most of these difficulties were occasioned by differing interpretations of the security problem and different priorities in the determination of policy. The United States concentrated on the need to strengthen Western military positions and the NATO defense structure as a means of meeting a threat from the Soviet Union. France was mainly concerned with its own more immediate interests of first combatting the nationalist movements in North Africa and then, after that struggle was lost, attempting to achieve a special relationship with them. France's establishment of close ties with Israel in the mid-1950s and then de Gaulle's abrupt shift to close ties with the Arab states were tactics aimed primarily at carving out gains for France outside the context of the main East-West equation.

During the period of de Gaulle, French policy in general—in the Mediterranean and Middle East as in Europe—was predicated upon France's status as a great power possessing nuclear weapons and upon the idea of a general compatibility of French and Soviet interests. Although France remained a party to the North Atlantic Treaty, it rejected the treaty's organized form, NATO, and sought détente with Moscow under which the two powers would consult on international questions and respect each other's interests. This was de Gaulle's way, without repudiating the American nuclear deterrent to war, of seeking a policy independent of the United States and of inducing the Soviets to favor the idea of a four-power "concert" in the Middle East and elsewhere. He sought to put French relations with Middle East countries on a new basis, shedding the close tie with the United States which was especially unpopular in many Arab countries.

The buildup of Soviet naval strength in the Mediterranean created a dilemma for the French. At first, they showed little concern and continued to keep large units of their navy in the Atlantic. In June

1968 they refused to approve a NATO Council resolution calling for greater allied efforts to meet the mounting Soviet threat in the Mediterranean. In November of the same year, however—after the Soviet invasion of Czechoslovakia—they subscribed to a NATO warning that any Soviet intervention in Europe or in the Mediterranean would cause an international crisis with serious consequences. French ships were redeployed to the Mediterranean and even participated in NATO maneuvers there.[9] This was no dramatic return to NATO but rather an indication that French naval policy is elastic. The professional naval officers generally favor cooperation with the United States, the government does not rule it out, and both can take comfort in the knowledge that their naval strength alone in the western Mediterranean outmatches that of the Soviets.[10] They seek to buttress their own positions, whether the fleets of the Big Two remain in the Mediterranean, which they know is almost inevitable, or whether they both get out, as Tunisia, Spain, Yugoslavia, and France itself have suggested.

With the flowering of East-West détente in the years since Pompidou replaced de Gaulle, France has contracted the scope of its ambitions and policies in more distant parts of the world, only to concentrate more heavily on a region close to home, the Mediterranean. The basic idea is that here France has a leading part to play because of its historic, political, and cultural ties with other littoral countries, its disinterested concern for their common security, its considerable commercial and financial interests, and its status as a permanent member of the U.N. Security Council. It has thus consistently sought to develop a policy of its own based to a large extent on political understanding and diplomacy.[11] Foreign Minister Maurice Schumann has said that France has but one aim: to prevent the western Mediterranean, and if possible the entire sea, from being a theater of cold war and a supplementary stake in the rivalry of great powers.[12] An oversimplification of French

9. Edward A. Kolodziej, "French Mediterranean Policy: The Politics of Weakness," *International Affairs*, July 1971, pp. 505–507.

10. René Mertens, "Naval Forces in the Mediterranean," in *Military Forces and Political Conflicts in the Mediterranean* (Paris: The Atlantic Institute, 1970), pp. 46–47.

11. Vincent Labouret, "Politique méditerranéenne de la France," *Politique Etrangère*, No. 5-6, 1971, pp. 489–99.

12. Ambassade de France, *Service de Presse et d'Information*, No. 1370, April 28, 1970, p. 8.

policy, perhaps, but a clear indication of official French thinking.

In the western Mediterranean France has attempted to take the leadership of such a movement through cooperation with Italy, Spain, and the states of the Maghreb. No treaty embracing these countries has emerged, but the French desire to lead such a grouping, wholly independent of NATO and with stress on nonalignment in the cold war, remains. In the eastern Mediterranean, this approach is centered on support of the Arab cause against Israel and denial of arms to the latter. It is evident also in French overtures to Greece and to Saudi Arabia and the deal to send over 100 *Mirage* planes to Libya. Should France have refused the Libyans' request, Schumann asked, and sentenced their country to "enfeoffment" as an "arena of rivalry between F5s, Migs, Chieftains, or Centurions?"[13]

The great obstacles for France have been its inability to wield influence comparable to that of the superpowers and its failure to gain notable support for its policies on either the northern or the southern shore. The littoral states realize that there is a big-power balance of which they have to take account whether they choose to lean to one side or stay in the middle. France does not have enough to offer either in security or in economic advantage. Italy and Spain have remained friendly but reserved, while Arab countries have gone along when French proposals were of benefit to them (e.g., arms deals) and balked when they appeared detrimental (e.g., Algeria's and Iraq's stand on oil).

Italy

Because of geography alone Italy is bound to be directly concerned with the maintenance of security in the Mediterranean, both eastern and western. It is heavily involved economically and has a vital interest in the freedom of transport in the inland sea and through its orifices at Gibraltar and Suez. The leaders of postwar Italy have had no thought of "mare nostrum," but they have seen the need to rebuild a respectable naval force which has its place in NATO's defense strategy and which the Soviets cannot ignore. Italy has been alarmed at the recent growth of Soviet naval power and especially at the possibility that the Soviets could get a foothold in Malta, Algeria, Albania, or Yugoslavia. The prospect is darkened by Italy's political weakness and the strength of the Italian Communist Party, which has been hammering at the NATO tie for over twenty years.

The Italian government, in contrast to certain politicians and special groups in Italy, has avoided stating a fixed or defined Mediterranean policy. It has supported recent NATO decisions and declarations but remains slightly distrustful of the American advocacy of increased allied naval strength because it seems to tie Italian and European interests to the purely American strategy of supporting Israel. Yet Italy has not followed the French lead toward a separate or neutral policy. Some politicians push the idea of a policy more independent of the United States, and they are not to be ignored since in this respect they are on the same wavelength as the communists.

To judge from recent initiatives taken in the European Economic Community, the Italians seem to be groping toward a Mediterranean policy for Europe that is not expressly tied to the balance between the United States and the Soviet Union, or to the Arab-Israel conflict. It is one which would follow neither Washington nor Paris but look to closer relations over the longer term with all the littoral states: in North Africa and the eastern Mediterranean, as well as in the Balkans.

The Federal Republic of Germany

Germany has had no military power in the Mediterranean and Middle East since the Second World War. Nevertheless, as a member of NATO and a country with growing economic power and political influence, the Federal Republic has developed interests in the area which inevitably create a concern for security. Danger comes from the increasing Soviet presence, from the Arab-Israel conflict which the German government would like to see peaceably settled, and from possible threats to Germany's oil supply. Foreign Minister Walter Scheel has spoken of the concern with which his government has watched the growing Soviet military power, especially in the Mediterranean, calling it an aggravating element in an already tense situation.[14] Germany has no naval units to throw into the breach, nor has it worked out a political strategy related to the balance of power in the Middle East. In this it can hardly act on its own and needs a common policy with NATO or European partners.

Meanwhile the Federal Republic's main attention has been directed to how its relationship with East Germany is affected by events in the region. The German Democratic Republic in its search for international recognition found the Middle East the most fertile ground in the world for undermining the Hallstein doctrine, especially after ten Arab coun-

13. Same, page 9.
14. Interview published in *Ha'aretz* of Tel Aviv, July 5, 1971.

tries broke relations with Bonn in 1965 because of its establishment of formal diplomatic ties with Israel.[15] In the future the question of East Germany's status will lose importance, and the Federal Republic should have a stronger inclination to redefine its own and Europe's interests. If and as the European Economic Community develops security policies of its own, Germany will be a constituent part of a Mediterranean power.

Japan

Japan's interest in security flows from its overwhelming dependence on Middle East oil. It wants to see stable conditions in the producing countries, so as to assure continued production of oil, and secure routes of transport across the Indian Ocean and through the Strait of Malacca. Its own military forces are too limited to have any capability to protect these interests either through naval deployment in the Indian Ocean or through a military backup of diplomacy. Although its admirals have already considered a naval force strong enough to protect merchant shipping going through the Strait of Malacca, if not by convoy then perhaps by a specialized attack force,[16] Japan's navy is now restricted to defense of the waters around the home islands. A possible alternative would be an agreed international regime for the strait.

Against a threat in the Middle East itself to the security of their oil supply, the Japanese have to rely primarily on the Western powers and on the Middle Eastern states to protect Japan's interests indirectly by protecting their own against Soviet encroachments or internal disturbances. But skillful oil diplomacy also has a role in seeing that relations with the local states are such as to shelter Japanese interests from the storms that batter those of other countries.

WHAT HAS BEEN DONE FOR THE COMMON SECURITY?

These various national interests and security considerations are on common ground in the need of all the advanced nations for (a) the avoidance of war; (b) continued access without interference to the Mediterranean–Middle East region for reasons of trade, transport, and communication, including access to oil; and (c) prevention of dominant Soviet influence. Views differ on how serious the threats to these interests are and what should or can be done, separately or together, to cope with them. For purposes of analysis the region can be looked at in two parts, west and east of Suez.

Under the defensive strategy developed after the Second World War the Western nations looked on security in the Mediterranean area as a necessary barrier both to Soviet penetration into the Middle East and Africa and to a Soviet flanking of Western Europe from the south. The former threat, evident even before the end of the war, mainly concerned the United States and Britain, the two powers with the greatest stake in Middle East oil and in a strategy of global containment. The latter concerned, in addition, most of the Mediterranean countries on the northern shore and some on the eastern and southern shores of that sea. From the time of the conclusion of the North Atlantic Treaty in 1949, which included the entire Mediterranean Sea and Algeria (then French) within the "treaty area," plans, deployments, and maneuvers have been undertaken for the defense of that area. Cyprus, Algeria, and Malta, on attaining independence, were excluded from the treaty's protection; but because Malta was the site of the headquarters of Allied Naval Forces, Southern Europe (now withdrawn at Malta's request) and of a British base used by NATO, and because Cyprus continued to have two British bases, those two islands have been, and remain, tied in with NATO's strategy though both of them now lean toward neutralism.[17]

As long as Soviet naval strength in the Mediterranean was negligible, the degree of coordination of NATO policy and strategy there was of limited importance. In 1956 the three principal Western powers felt

15. Inge Deutschkron, *Bonn and Jerusalem: The Strange Coalition* (Philadelphia: Chilton Book Company, 1970), pp. 306–32.
16. Takashi Oka, in *The New York Times*, August 20, 1969.
17. The recent diplomatic tempest over Malta developed from Prime Minister Dom Mintoff's demand for a higher rent for the base, accompanied by a threat that he would kick the British out if they refused. They did and he did. But then other NATO powers entered the scene, and Joseph Luns, NATO Secretary General, took part in subsequent negotiations. Not that the facilities were so important to the British or to NATO; the real concern was over the military and psychological effects of their becoming available to the Soviet navy if the British left. Although at first the affair was handled on the Western side with a notable lack of skill, the common Western interest finally made itself felt, and an agreement was reached on March 26, 1972. See "Malta e l'equilibrio politico-strategico del Mediterraneo," *Relazioni Internazionali*, February 12, 1972, pp. 155 ff.

free to indulge in the luxury of conflicting policies in the crisis over Suez. For the next decade the U.S. Sixth Fleet remained the dominant naval force in the Mediterranean. None of the Western allies worried about any outside challenge to that situation, although one of them, France, chafed under the fact of its dependence. With the appearance and growth of a significant Soviet naval force in the Mediterranean from the mid-1960s onward, the United States and other NATO members urged that countermeasures be taken to increase the alliance's naval strength and coordination. At Reykjavik in June 1968, the NATO ministers (with the specific exception of their French colleague) agreed that measures should be taken to safeguard their countries' security interests in the Mediterranean and to improve the effectiveness of allied forces.[18] In November 1968, NATO set up a new command, Maritime Air Forces, Mediterranean (Marairmed), based in Naples, for coordinated surveillance. American, British, and Italian units, in it from the start, were later joined by those of Greece and Turkey. In the same month the NATO ministers at Brussels called for further vigilance and directly warned the Soviets against any intervention directly or indirectly affecting the situation in the Mediterranean.[19] In 1969, the United States, Britain, and Italy (later joined by Greece and Turkey) earmarked ships from their national naval forces in the area to provide the nucleus of a NATO force which would come together for maneuvers, visits, training, and in time of tension for possible operations. The call to vigilance goes forth from each succeeding NATO conference, but no actual agreements on further buildup and coordination of Western naval forces have been made.[20] Meanwhile, the Americans and British have added slightly to the strength and modernization of their forces there.

East of Suez it is a different story. The area is larger; the military forces involved are smaller; the confrontation of great powers is not so intense. The intrusion of Soviet power has been confined to the threat of direct attack from the north, occasional visits of naval vessels to Persian Gulf ports, increasing maritime interests and a more or less permanent small naval force in the Indian Ocean, and the presumed availability of naval and air facilities in Southern Yemen, Somalia, Iraq, India, and elsewhere. Here there is no NATO to plan and coordinate an effective strategy for Western security. CENTO is but a pale imitation, with a weaker basis of commitment and no standing forces at its disposal. Great Britain, CENTO's only Western member, has cast doubt on the value of its imprecise treaty obligation by washing its hands of any major military role east of Suez, and the United States has helped to downgrade the organization by not joining it although participating in many of its functions. Turkey looks to NATO rather than CENTO for security, and Pakistan can be written off.

That leaves Iran as a keystone of the Western position in the area of the Gulf, an obstacle to Soviet territorial access to Arab client states and to the southern seas, and a factor of stability amid the rivalries and turmoil of the region. That is precisely the role the Shah envisages for his country. Whereas in the early postwar years Iran needed Western guarantees and help, it is now the Western nations which are more in need of a strong Iran. Hence the large American and British programs for the sale of military equipment to that country. Hence Britain's "collusion" in Iran's seizure of strategically located islands in the Hormuz Strait before the termination of British defense obligations to the Arab Trucial States at the end of 1971. The U.S. security agreement with Iran, concluded in 1959, remains an element in the balance of deterrence, but a more important one is Iran's own strength and progress. The Shah insists that Iran be independent. He wants no junior partnership with American or other foreign naval forces in the Gulf, but a leading role for Iran. At the moment he plays the game with remarkable success and confidence, but his own future and that of his country are clouded with uncertainties.

With Britain's decision to withdraw, the Soviet naval presence and potential threat in the Indian Ocean, Persian Gulf, and Red Sea have become, as noted earlier, an American rather than a general Western concern. What are the alternatives for a specifically American policy? The first reaction to the new situation was to urge the British to stay, with some financial support from the United States. But even with the advent of the Heath government, London did not change its mind about withdrawing from the Persian Gulf—although it did about Singa-

18. *Final Communiqué*, Department of State Press Release, No. 148, June 26, 1968.
19. *Final Communiqué*, Department of State Press Release, No. 259, November 18, 1968.
20. Secretary Laird, who had previously cited the Soviet deployment of Mig 23s in Egypt as adversely affecting the balance between Soviet and NATO forces, proposed in December 1971 the formation of a permanent allied force of American, British, Italian, Greek, and Turkish vessels in the eastern Mediterranean (*The New York Times*, December 9, 1971).

pore and, in addition, plans to retain facilities in Oman and at Gan (in the Maldives). The second reaction was to consider acquiring one or more bases from which the United States itself could exert power in the region, but nothing was done beyond an arrangement with the British (December 1970) to develop on Diego Garcia what the U.S. government describes as an "austere communications facility," which presumably could become a more elaborate base if need be.[21] The third choice was to go along with things as they are, keeping the low profile favored by the Nixon Administration.

A State Department officer put it this way in 1971:

> ... we cannot assign a single value to the totality of our interests in the Indian Ocean. Nevertheless, we do consider that over the next five years our interests there will be of a substantially lower order than those in either of the great ocean basins, the Atlantic and the Pacific. We border on the Atlantic and the Pacific, and the states of these areas are for the most part economically, politically, and militarily more important to us than those on the Indian Ocean. Therefore, there appears to be no requirement at this time for us to feel impelled to control, or even decisively influence, any part of the Indian Ocean or its littoral, given the nature of our interests there and the current level of Soviet and Chinese involvement. We consider, on balance, that our present interests are served by normal commercial, political, and military access.[22]

In actuality the profile is not so low as these words suggest. The small U.S. naval force of two destroyers and a tender (Mideastfor), now based at Bahrain under an agreement with that country, remains and may be strengthened and modernized. The Navy Department announced in September 1971 that the Seventh Fleet would begin sending more ships into the Indian Ocean in response to Soviet moves. And after the Indian-Pakistani war the following December, during which the United States sent a Seventh Fleet task force into the Bay of Bengal, the Department of Defense expressed a growing interest in the strategic importance of the Indian Ocean, and announced that the Navy would conduct periodic operations "to help establish an American presence . . . now that the British have withdrawn."[23]

A game of reciprocal buildup and balance is being played. Probably neither Moscow nor Washington wishes to see the commitment of forces climb very high, for the potential gains through doing so are far from apparent. Itinerant naval units, especially if the two sides are in rough balance, are hardly going to exercise significant influence on the littoral states. As for China, a common rival of both, it has no naval force present, but does not neglect political opportunities in its verbal support to the peoples of the region in their struggle against the "American imperialists" and the "Soviet revisionist social-imperialists."[24]

21. This was done under the so-called "BIOT Agreement" between the United Kingdom and the United States (December 1966) by which transit and other facilities were to be developed jointly in the British Indian Ocean Territories.

22. Ronald I. Spiers, "U.S. National Security Policy and the Indian Ocean Area," *The Department of State Bulletin*, August 23, 1971, p. 203.

23. *The New York Times*, September 29, 1971; January 7, 1972.

24. "U.S.-Soviet Scramble for Hegemony in South Asian Subcontinent and Indian Ocean," *Peking Review*, January 14, 1972, pp. 16–17.

II.

POLITICS: THE ARAB-ISRAEL CONFLICT

The case of Greece and Turkey illustrates the relationship of security to politics and economics. The two countries, though full partners in NATO, for years saw their security problems in a somewhat different light from the Western European members. Indeed, their status was not far from that of military wards of the United States. To them, NATO's real meaning was the American guarantee and American arms. Western Europe's military power did not loom large enough at the eastern end of the Mediterranean at a time of direct danger from the Soviet Union and its faithful ally, Bulgaria.

Developments of recent years have now changed the picture considerably: Moscow has practiced détente with Greece and Turkey as well as with the West, and the tension has relaxed; local economic and cultural arrangements in the Balkan area have drawn together the two NATO members, several states of the Warsaw Pact, and nonaligned Yugoslavia; the United States has talked of lowering its military posture, has diminished its military and economic aid to Turkey, and has had trouble, amid conflicting attitudes and pressures, in finding its way to a consistent policy toward Greece.

To the extent that security problems are eased, political and economic factors come to the fore. The attention of Greeks and Turks has turned more toward relations with each other, especially over the unsettled and dangerous Cyprus dispute, and toward the great economic unit that has emerged in Western Europe. The E.E.C. is their main trading partner, and both countries have negotiated an association with it. Europe thus returns to a cooperative role in the eastern Mediterranean that has no resemblance to old imperial relationships. Little may be said on either side about NATO and military commitments; the military problem for Greeks and Turks, despite détente, is still one of danger from Russia and protection provided by America. In the long run, however, Europe's new influence should alter the way in which Greece, Turkey, and other nations of the eastern Mediterranean see their political and security interests as well as their economic concerns.

Today, of course, the center of political strife in the Middle East lies in the Arab-Israel zone, where the cold war has persisted as it has melted into détente elsewhere. It is almost entirely a Soviet-American contest, with each superpower trying to check the moves of the other, America's NATO allies keeping their distance, and Japan staying clear altogether. The Soviet-American competition, moreover, is tied to the local conflict to a dangerous degree. In 1947 the two powers were together in supporting the partition of Palestine and the independence of Israel. In 1956 they were again together, by circumstance rather than by design, in condemning the Israeli invasion of Egypt and insisting on total withdrawal of Israel's troops from all conquered territory. In taking the postwar period as a whole, however, these momentary alignments are deceiving. The two powers did not cease to follow strategies directed against each other even when for tactical or other reasons they found themselves on the same side.

THE DIPLOMACY OF THE UNITED STATES

American policy toward the Arab lands has been motivated for the most part by general considerations reaching well beyond the Mediterranean–Middle East region. The basic idea was to check the expansion of Soviet power, in this as in other regions, and to do so with as much cooperation as possible from Western allies and from the local peoples. In practice, neither played the game in this area as we intended they should. The process of decolonization was too violent and too unpredictable to be managed or controlled by the United States, and association with former colonial powers often increased the difficulties. Despite American denunciations of colonialism and generous aid programs to strengthen the independence of recipient nations, real cooperation with the United States was not a paying proposition for most Arab politicians in an age of nationalism, only for those rulers whose personal or financial stake in the American connection was great enough to guarantee their alignment. The Soviet Union, once it established itself as a power in the region in the middle 1950s, had a good deal more success than the United States in turning local forces, trends, and ambitions to its own advantage.

The main reason for the difference is the obvious one, Israel. American support of Israel in its early years grew out of a number of currents in American life, humanitarian and sentimental and electoral. At the heart of it has been the abiding identification with Israel's cause on the part of a large body of American Jews who have exercised an influence beyond their numbers. But the American commitment and support is not explained by Jewish influence or political pressure alone.

The need of Europe's surviving Jews for a refuge after the Second World War, admiration for Israel's fight for independence and later accomplishments, and the war of 1967 all contributed to pro-Israel sentiment.

Since the presidency of Harry Truman, Israel has had fairly consistent support in the White House, in the Congress, and in the organs of the press. This choice was at first opposed, deplored, and only reluctantly accepted by many officials in the Departments of State and Defense on the grounds that it jeopardized Arab cooperation in defense and possibly also Western access to Middle East oil. Over the years, successive U.S. administrations attempted to escape from this dilemma by pronouncements of impartiality between the Arab states and Israel, by trying to make the armistice agreements work, and by seeking practical ways toward improved relations and eventual peace. The results were meager. The obstacles to cooperation with Egypt and other Arab states which followed a similar course of radical, anti-Western nationalism were big enough anyway, wholly aside from the question of Israel.

The war of 1967 served to underline some of the old elements in the equation and also to introduce new ones. The United States found itself more than ever on the outs with the Arabs, who associated this country with Israel's victory and with Arab humiliation. American attempts to promote a fair settlement through the United Nations won no Arab plaudits when Washington took a firm stand against unconditional Israeli withdrawal from the occupied territories as the precondition or sole test of settlement. More than before the war, the Soviet Union was the political beneficiary of the American association with Israel.

The United States has manfully tried to bring Egypt and Israel together to find a solution on the basis of U.N. Security Council Resolution 242. In December 1969 Secretary Rogers laid out U.S. views on the outlines of a fair settlement in more specific terms than ever before, including acceptance of the armistice lines as permanent frontiers except for agreed minor modifications.[25] More recently American diplomacy has tried to bring about an interim settlement covering the Suez Canal. Cairo and Amman have been willing to listen. But all such efforts suffer from the same old handicap, the inability of Washington to deliver Israel's agreement to the proposition that the terms of settlement will include withdrawal from all or virtually all occupied territory. The most telling illustration came in February 1971 when Israel could not be persuaded to yield on that point after Egypt, in response to a direct question from U.N. Representative Gunnar Jarring, had stated its willingness to conclude a "peace agreement" with Israel.

The new element is a result of Israel's military prowess, demonstrated by the war and by the continued development of its forces and armaments ever since. For several reasons, including the continued shipments of arms to Egypt, the Soviet military presence in that country through its thousands of advisers and combat personnel, and the general buildup of Soviet power in the Mediterranean, the United States has come to regard Israel as an essential factor in the balance of power and in the prevention of a new local or even a wider war. In practice that has meant that the existing balance, reflecting Israel's superiority over all the Arab armies, will be maintained by American shipments of arms to Israel to offset Soviet deliveries to Arab states. At a time when the U.S. government is preaching the doctrine of reducing commitments and letting other countries do their own fighting with American arms without calling on American troops, this is a congenial policy. But a policy of counting on Israel as important to American security makes the parallel policy of persuading Israel to be more flexible on terms of settlement seem a little hollow.

American diplomacy probably could not bring Israel to return to the old armistice lines even if it could bring itself to apply economic pressure or could offer ironclad guarantees against violation of the ensuing settlement. The argument that the United States is in a uniquely favorable position to bring the parties to a settlement rests on dubious assumptions, though it remains true that no other outside powers are in any better position, simply because they have no influence with Israel and cannot get it without losing what influence they have with the Arabs. Meanwhile the lack of a settlement and the ever-present danger of war continue to trouble relations among the Western powers and to maintain tensions between America and Russia. As the focus here is on the Western nations, let us look at their differences before exploring whether there is anything useful they can do together.

25. Speech of December 9, 1969, *The Department of State Bulletin*, January 5, 1970, pp. 7–11. On frontiers in general, Rogers stated that the armistice lines should become permanent borders, subject to "insubstantial alterations required for mutual security." He implied in a separate statement on settlement between Egypt and Israel that Egypt's permanent frontier should be the historic Palestine-Egyptian border.

THE POLICIES OF WESTERN NATIONS

Great Britain

During the 1960s, Britain took no lead in dealing with the Arab-Israel conflict, reflecting its concentration on the region east of Suez. It had no interests and influence in Israel comparable to those of the United States; and in Egypt, where it had never recovered from the Suez affair in 1956, it had the added handicap of embroilment in Yemen and Aden where Nasser's ambitions lay. As the great-power competition in the Arab-Israel area became almost exclusively a matter for the United States and the Soviet Union, the British held back, husbanding what little diplomatic capital they had.

Then came 1967. Britain counseled peace to both sides during the crisis of May and took part in the attempt to organize the maritime powers to support Israel's right to navigation through the Strait of Tiran, but in neither respect was its diplomacy effective (nor was that of anybody else). After the war, London vigorously supported the idea of a comprehensive settlement in which both sides would make concessions: Israel on withdrawal and on the Arab refugees; the Arab states on recognition, the end of belligerency, and freedom of navigation. In the U.N. General Assembly Britain voted against the draft resolutions for unconditional Israeli withdrawal, and Lord Caradon's dexterous diplomacy in the Security Council finally brought about unanimous agreement on the famous Resolution 242 of November 22, 1967.

It was not long, however, before the British were taking positions that alienated Israel. They supported Arab complaints to the Security Council on such sensitive subjects as Jerusalem. They condemned Israel's massive raids against targets in Jordan and Lebanon. They refused to sell Chieftain tanks to Israel while selling them to Arab countries. Britain was not doing anything for Israel economically that might counterbalance these pro-Arab gestures. On the other hand, although London was able to renew diplomatic relations with Cairo (in November 1967), it could gain little leverage there because it was not ready to accept Egypt's interpretation of Resolution 242 and would not move very far from American positions.

The Wilson government (especially Foreign Secretary George Brown and the old Middle East hands at the Foreign Office) was not particularly sympathetic to Israel's policies, and the Conservative government which came into power in 1970 was even less so. Sir Alec Douglas-

Home, in a policy speech later that year, took a position on peace terms not very different from those outlined by Secretary Rogers in December 1969. The basis was the inadmissibility of the acquisition of territory by war and the necessity of a just and lasting peace in which each state could live in security. He said the boundaries should be negotiated by the parties but then went on to state his belief that the old international frontier (which was also the armistice line) should be the boundary between Israel and Egypt, that there might be agreed minor changes in the armistice line between Israel and Jordan, and (avoiding specificity) that the same considerations should apply to the Israel-Syria boundary as to the others although Syria had never accepted Resolution 242. He made clear, however, that Israel's acceptance of such terms required pledges and guarantees of the new borders.[26]

The speech caused bitterness in Israel where it was taken as a pro-Arab statement and proof that Britain no longer was sympathetic to Israeli interests or even in a middle or neutral position. The Israelis tend to see the four-power forum as a loaded 3–to–1 lineup against them. The British have stuck to their position, and Douglas-Home recently restated it, praising Egypt's willingness to reach a peace agreement and putting the burden on Israel to agree to full withdrawal from Egypt.[27] The fact that the speech was made in Cairo and stressed Egypt's real will for peace added insult to what Israel felt was already repeated injury. In contrast, the impression was created, in Egypt anyway, that Britain's position had become more favorable to the Arab view than it was before.

While there is no official policy statement to prove it, the British might well go along with the idea of world pressure on Israel to accept the principle of withdrawal to the old armistice lines now that Egypt has expressed willingness to sign a peace agreement. As for the proposed interim settlement involving partial Israeli withdrawal and reopening of the Suez Canal, London favors it both for commercial reasons and on political grounds as a concrete step toward peace.

France

President de Gaulle's turn from a de facto alliance with Israel to a pro-Arab policy was in accord with his concept of an independent policy for France in the Middle East as elsewhere. Even before the war of 1967

26. Speech at Harrogate, November 2, 1970, excerpts in *The Times*, November 6, 1970.
27. *The Times*, September 14, 1971.

he had dissociated France from American and NATO policies in the Mediterranean, sought a new postcolonial relationship with the countries of the Maghreb, and tried to make arrangements with several Arab governments on arms and on oil. Where the war in Algeria had brought France and Israel together in the 1950s, de Gaulle's decisions to end the war and to make Algeria the centerpiece of a new policy toward Africa and the Middle East were, for France, a natural return to historic interests. Their effect was immediately evident in French-Israeli relations.[28]

Israel's effrontery in disobeying de Gaulle's advice not to start the shooting in June 1967 gave him an issue on which to base a policy of cutting down deliveries of arms to Israel (even 50 *Mirages* already paid for) and to espouse the Arab position on Israeli withdrawal from occupied territories. The Israeli raid on the Beirut airport in December 1968 angered him to the point of making the ban on arms a total one.

On every possible occasion following the war de Gaulle proposed and backed the idea of a Big-Four approach to settlement, so as to assure France's right to an equal voice with the United States, Britain, and the Soviet Union. In the four-power talks on the Middle East at the United Nations, France attempted to get agreement on compromises somewhere between the American and Soviet positions, but with no great success. When the United States tried a new route in June 1970, by taking the initiative with the "Rogers plan" for a cease-fire on the Suez front, the Soviet Union was kept informed and gave its general assent, but France was not consulted and was not associated with the project in any way. Pompidou said at that time, "There is no French plan for a settlement and there must not be an American plan . . . nor a Soviet plan . . . It is necessary that the four powers present a common plan."[29]

The transition from de Gaulle to Pompidou brought the end of the situation in which the head of state displayed a personal animus against the Jews in general, and was also marked by a slight easement of France's tough attitude toward Israel, but the basic policies remained unchanged. Foreign Minister Schumann, in describing France's policy for peace, stated that the essential condition was the evacuation of the occupied territories, whatever might be the guarantees and arrangements for keeping the peace.[30] In fact, the French desire for a leading role in the Mediterranean region could only be satisfied with the cooperation of Arab governments. Hence the maintenance of the ban on arms to Israel, the delay on Israel's application to the E.E.C. for more favorable trade terms, negotiations on oil and on arms with a number of Arab states (both radical and conservative), expansion of trade with them, and the promotion of flourishing cultural relations especially with Algeria, Tunisia, and Morocco.

Against the potential commercial and political gains with the Arabs, France saw nothing comparable in relations with Israel; in fact, bad relations with Israel were a necessary part of the strategy with the Arabs. It was the French purpose that France should appear in Arab eyes as the only Western power with an independent and fair policy on the Arab-Israel conflict, not aligned with the United States or with Israel. Consistent with the policy of being out in front of other Western nations in cultivating détente with Moscow, Pompidou declared in the presence of Leonid Brezhnev in October 1971 that French policy in the Middle East was close to that of the Soviet Union, and on important points, identical.[31]

The real question about French policy, as indicated earlier in the discussion of security and military strategy, was whether it would produce the desired results, whether the pro-Arab line on the Arab-Israel conflict and such moves as the arms deal with Libya could significantly increase French influence on the course of events in the Mediterranean and Middle East. It was at least a plausible argument that by its independent stance France offered the Arab states an alternative to the superpowers and could provide a Western connection for the Arabs at a time when the United States, with its favoritism toward Israel, could not. The main obstacle to success was that while Arab governments appreciated French support, France did not have the military or political power to get them what they wanted from Israel. French cultural influence was not translatable into political gains; and the idea of a Mediterranean for the Mediterranean peoples, excluding the superpowers, was not sufficiently realistic to the Arab states in the eastern Mediterranean which depended on the U.S.S.R. for support against

28. André Fontaine, "Pompidou's Mediterranean Policy," *Interplay*, April 1970, p. 13; Paul Balta, "La France et le monde arabe," *Revue de Défense Nationale*, May 1970, pp. 769–779, and June 1970, pp. 924–34.

29. Press conference, July 2, 1970 (Ambassade de France, *Service de Presse et d'Information*, No. 1413).

30. Paul Balta, cited, p. 929.

31. Address delivered on October 25, 1971 (Ambassade de France, *Service de Presse et d'Information*, No. 71/189).

Israel, nor to those in the Maghreb which sought a greater independence for themselves. Yet France's approach cannot be airily dismissed, for it contains elements that may have value to other Western nations.

The Federal Republic of Germany

The Federal Republic, not considered a Mediterranean or Middle East power on its own and not yet a member of the United Nations, has not been in the forefront of efforts either to gain advantage from the Arab-Israel conflict or to bring about a settlement. Yet it has not been free of that conflict's consequences.

Beginning in the early 1950s, West Germany developed a special relationship with Israel based at first on the concept of reparation and restitution. In 1952 the Bonn government agreed to pay a large sum (DM 3,450 million) to Israel over a twelve-year period.[32] In addition, at the meeting of Konrad Adenauer and David Ben-Gurion in New York in 1960, agreement was reached in principle on regular economic aid, which was eventually extended, and is still continuing, in a series of low-interest loans for specific projects to a total of about $35 million annually. West Germany also provided military aid to Israel, apparently from the late 1950s; before it was abruptly suspended in 1965 under pressure from the Arabs, it had reached an amount which was probably well over the $80 million nominal value assigned to it.[33]

Some of the German military aid to Israel took the form of significant quantities of U.S. equipment, including tanks, which became surplus as the U.S. military aid program for Germany continued. These deliveries, undertaken largely because the United States itself did not want to provide equipment directly to Israel, got the Germans into political trouble when certain Arab states raised a fuss about the arms shipments and threatened reprisals against Bonn. The German government chose to end the military program but at the same time to establish formal relations with Israel. The Arab states were happy about the first decision but so angry over the second that ten of them broke their own diplomatic relations with Bonn. They did not immediately recognize the German Democratic Republic, however, as they were anxious not to lose their important economic ties with the Federal Republic. The latter, to counter the effects of its massive aid to Israel and to build up commercial and other ties, had extended large credits to a number of Arab states as well.

Several Arab states which broke with Bonn in 1965 later renewed ties, and the Arab League has taken the position that any member may do the same in its own good time. Egypt, the key country, has good reason to renew relations because, as the journalist, Mohammed Hassanayn Haykal, has said, absence from "the German front" has only served to hurt the Arab economies and to help Israel's.[34]

Israel has naturally done what it could to make the "special" Bonn-Jerusalem relations, the heritage of the Hitler regime and of Adenauer's statesmanship, special in regard to the conflict with the Arabs, but the Germans have been careful to avoid commitments and to stress the normal character of relations. When Foreign Minister Eban visited Germany in February 1970, he took pains to underline the "special ties," recognized by all German governments from Adenauer on, and his conviction that the Federal Republic would not be neutral on such a question as Israel's right to exist.[35] His German counterpart, Walter Scheel, on the other hand, noted that a settlement of the Arab-Israel conflict should be on the basis of Resolution 242, and that while Israel was of course a party to the conflict, Germany was in the position of an observer. In the summer of 1971 when Scheel visited Israel, the public statements took the same line. He spoke of Germany's endeavors to pursue "a balanced policy" in the Middle East, including an improvement of relations with the Arab states in order to protect its interests in the region as a whole, but added that this would not be done at Israel's expense. As for the achievement of a peaceful settlement, the Federal Republic would support all efforts to that end, but there was not much that it could itself contribute. At the same time a German press officer stated that his government did not believe that Resolution 242 required Israel's total withdrawal from occupied territories.[36]

The European Economic Community

Other West European countries have been less interested in the Arab-Israel conflict and have succeeded in keeping out of it. Yet almost all

32. Agreement between the State of Israel and the Federal Republic of Germany, signed at Luxembourg on 10 September 1952. Text of treaty and related documents in United Nations, *Treaty Series*, Volume 162, 1953, pp. 206–311.

33. J. C. Hurewitz, *Middle East Politics: The Military Dimension* (New York: Praeger, 1968), p. 477; Nadav Safran, *From War to War: The Arab-Israeli Confrontation 1948–1967*, (New York: Pegasus, 1969), pp. 167–69.

34. *Al Ahram*, November 16, 1971 (broadcast by Cairo Radio).

35. Interview in *Die Welt*, February 25, 1970.

36. *Ha'aretz*, July 5, 1971; Jerusalem radio service, July 8, 1971.

have had the same combination of public sympathy toward Israel and economic interests in the Arab states which exists in France and Germany. All members of the E.E.C. have felt the need, moreover, to do something on behalf of peace in the area in order to be able to further their common interests in economic relations both with Israel and with the Arab states. This has been especially true of Italy, which has managed to have good relations and trade with both sides and has generally preached détente and settlement. During the course of 1970 and 1971, high officials of all member states visited Israel or major Arab states to get information, make contacts, and explore the possibilities of diplomacy.

Because of this obvious interest, it was natural, though much too ambitious, for the six governments to take the Middle East as one of the first two subjects on which to try, under the Davignon Plan, to reach a generally agreed foreign policy. It was discussed by the ministers of the Six at Munich in November 1970 among themselves and then, "for information," with representatives of the United Kingdom and the other three candidate states. A group of experts from the foreign ministries of the Six then prepared a paper on which the foreign ministers agreed at their meeting in Paris in May 1971. The paper was not made public but was reported in the press as including the following points: withdrawal of Israeli forces to the old armistice lines, which would be the new frontiers; stationing of international forces on both sides of those frontiers; the "administrative internationalization" of Jerusalem; a choice for Palestinian refugees to return to their homes or to receive compensation; freedom of navigation through the Suez Canal; and the urgency of reaching a peace settlement through the Jarring mission on the basis of Resolution 242.[37]

It was no surprise that this paper, or rumors of what it contained, stirred up Israeli objections to "this unfortunate and untimely document." It looked to the Israelis as if France had simply sold its own policy to the other members.[38] That was one reason why Scheel was pressed hard, when he visited Israel in July, to re-emphasize Germany's special relationship with Israel and its nonacceptance of the E.E.C. paper. Scheel would not repudiate it, but he did point out that it was a working paper and not a policy declaration, that it was generally based on a U.N. resolution which Israel itself had accepted, and that there was no common interpretation of it. Foreign Minister Pierre Harmel of Belgium made the same points when he visited Israel at the end of July.[39]

Thus, while there was some pussyfooting on the part of individual governments under pressure of one kind or another, all of them chose not to break the solidarity among themselves that they had established through beginning to discuss areas of possible common policy; and they were not pleased that Israel had raised such a row about it. They recognized they were at an early stage of the experiment and that much patience and tenacity would be necessary to carry it out. Subsequent lack of progress indicates how tough a test case the E.E.C. governments had chosen for their first effort toward an agreed foreign policy.

WHAT BASIS FOR A COMMON POLICY?

An attempt to answer this question requires moving beyond U.N. Resolution 242, which all concerned—the United States and all the Western European states, to say nothing of the U.S.S.R., the principal Arab states, and Israel—have in one form or another accepted. The real questions, as the E.E.C. paper recognized, concern what should actually be done about withdrawal of Israeli forces, definitive frontiers, demilitarization, international peacekeeping forces, guarantees, and the fate of Palestinian refugees. Additionally, the Western powers, even if they can agree on desirable terms, have the problems of resolving their differences in approach to the two sides, deciding what pressure, if any, to bring to bear on them, and making up their minds on how to deal with the Soviet Union.

From the positions taken by the Western governments since the war of 1967, individually or collectively, one point stands out. There is no

37. *Europe,* Agence internationale d'information pour la presse, November 19, 20, December 2, 1970, May 13, 14, 1971; *Le Monde,* May 14, 1971.

38. According to French Foreign Minister Maurice Schumann, France had indeed first proposed the subject at the E.E.C. ministerial meeting and he, in raising it, had referred to the diverging positions taken on the Middle East by member governments at the U.N. General Assembly and urged them to seek a basis for agreement on various aspects important to a possible settlement. He mentioned specifically the same points that appeared later in the E.E.C. paper, including, "to our great satisfaction," the Palestinian problem. See Schumann's statement before the French Senate, November 30, 1970 (Ambassade de France, *Service de Presse et d'Information,* No. 1492, pp. 8–10).

39. *The Jerusalem Post,* August 3, 1971.

major difference on the key issue of where the "secure and agreed" final boundaries should run. France says they should be identical with the pre-1967 armistice lines, which, except in the case of the Israel-Jordan line, were the old boundaries of the British Palestine mandate. The other members of the Six, by their approval of the famous "working paper," appear to hold the same view, although this conclusion is subject to confirmation by more explicit and official statements of governments. The British and American governments have taken the same position, with the exception that they believe that mutually agreed minor rectifications of the long and wriggly Israel-Jordan line may be desirable. They have also refrained from being specific about the Israel-Syria line in the absence of Syrian acceptance of Resolution 242.

That resolution and most of the Western nations' statements of national policy based on it link withdrawal of occupying forces with the right of all states to live at peace within secure and recognized boundaries. Because these two principles were considered as rights valid in themselves, they were not expressed as a bargain or an exchange. Nevertheless the Western governments, like Ambassador Jarring, tended to look on them as interdependent and as the heart of the whole package that would form the peace settlement. The United States and Britain, for example, were for a long time critical of Israel for not accepting the principle of withdrawal as a necessary part of a political settlement, and of the Arab states for insisting there could be no treaty with Israel. Consequently, when the U.A.R. stated in a memorandum to Jarring early in 1971 that Egypt was prepared to sign a "peace agreement" with Israel once the latter had given commitments on total withdrawal and negotiated agreement on other matters, the burden was on Israel to make a comparable concession on withdrawal. Israel's reply to Jarring, in the view of the Western powers, was not responsive, for Mrs. Meir's government went out of its way to state bluntly that "Israel will not return to the armistice lines of June 4, 1967."[40]

The three major Western powers reacted to the situation along familiar lines. France commended Sadat's reasonableness and saw the need for the application of pressure to reduce Israel's intransigence, but knew that only the United States could apply pressure with any hope of success. The British were more or less of the same opinion. The United States tried diplomatic persuasion with a view to getting Israel to soften its position at least to the point of making it possible to reactivate the Jarring mission, but with no success despite visits of high American officials to Cairo, Amman, and Jerusalem.

While the matter of a comprehensive settlement has been in limbo, efforts of U.S. diplomacy to bring about a limited agreement involving withdrawal of Israeli forces to a new line in Sinai and reopening of the Suez Canal have drawn concrete proposals from both sides but, as yet, no concessions sufficient to indicate a real possibility of compromise. The British have given nominal support; the French none. Consequently, since the gap between Egyptian and Israeli positions remains unbridged, the United States has the onus of another diplomatic failure, and the Western European countries can point again to American reluctance to press Israel to make concessions.

The episode illustrates the fundamental difficulty of attaining a degree of Western solidarity which will be effective in bringing the parties to a settlement. None has much leverage with Egypt, which can always turn to the Soviet side for support. Only the United States has influence with Israel, but the record of the past year has shown that neither diplomatic argument nor varying tactics in meeting requests for arms is sufficient to cause Israel to alter its basic policies, which are backed by strong convictions. American tactics have annoyed Israel without changing its policies. The United States has not been prepared to exercise stronger types of suasion and is not sure they would work.[41]

It is well to understand American reluctance by recalling the context of security and the balance of Soviet and American power. It is not just a question of a Zionist lobby or of the influence of the American Jewish community in domestic politics. Those factors are present, especially in a presidential election year. More important now is the place of Israel in American calculations on the balance of power in the Middle East. With the increasing Soviet military presence in the Mediterranean and in Arab countries at odds with Israel, the United States has come, rightly or wrongly, to regard Israel's ability to hold its own in the face of an Arab-Soviet military position as a vital American interest. Presidential statements to the effect that we will not permit the balance to be tipped against Israel, which seems in fact to mean no change in the situation of Israeli superiority that has existed since the 1967 war, commit the United States to matching, through arms deliveries to Israel,

40. The Jarring memorandum, dated February 8, 1971, and Egypt's and Israel's replies, dated February 15 and 26, 1971, respectively, have been issued as United Nations Document A/8541–S/10403, on November 30, 1971.

41. John C. Campbell, "Is America's Lone Hand Played Out?" *New Middle East*, September 1971, pp. 11–15.

each increase in strength of the Arab-Soviet position in Egypt and Syria. In like manner the pleas of Senator Jackson and others in Congress for large-scale arms shipments to Israel reflect a strong concern for America's as well as for Israel's security.

The force of this point of view, added to the general current of pro-Israel sentiment in the Congress, makes it very difficult for the State Department, if it were so minded, to use the arms-supply question as a means of influence on Israeli policies. Actually, the Department has seemed more partial to the idea that if Israel gets the arms it wants, it will feel secure and thus better able to make concessions. These factors make virtually impossible anything in the way of economic or other real pressures on Israel to soften its policies. In turn, this inability to move Israel deprives the United States of its leverage in asking for concessions on the part of Arab states.

III.

ECONOMICS: PETROLEUM

Oil is by far the major economic interest of the advanced industrial nations in the Middle East and North Africa. That area, especially the Persian Gulf region, is the world's great reservoir of oil, with some two-thirds of the proven reserves. Its oil is cheap to produce, easy to transport. Indeed, it is hard to find words which would exaggerate its importance as long as demand for energy moves dramatically upward and no real substitutes for petroleum are found to fill that demand.

Projections of demand through the 1970s made by the Organization of Economic Cooperation and Development are as follows:

	1970	1975	1980
		(millions of metric tons)	
North America	775	920	up to 1,100
Western Europe (O.E.C.D.)	600	850	up to 1,200
Japan	175	300	up to 510
Total	1,550	2,070	up to 2,810

The figures for the future, of course, are estimates and not yet verifiable fact; data for 1971 already indicate a rate of demand somewhat less than expected. But there is no doubt of the great quantities of oil that will be needed and of the importance of the question: From where can this oil come? The United States now supplies 80 per cent of its needs from domestic sources and imports less than 5 per cent from the Middle East. At present rates of production, however, its proven reserves, which have been declining since 1967, would last no more than ten to twelve years. The North Slope of Alaska will add some 10 billion to 15 billion barrels of reserves; but, even with those and with oil available from Canada, the trend will be one of increasing dependence on oil from outside North America. Estimates based on the continuance of current policies and price levels indicate that by 1980 the United States will need to import perhaps 25 per cent of its oil requirements from the Eastern Hemisphere.[42] Some experts place the dependence on imported oil or gas at a considerably higher level.

42. Henry B. Steele and Dankwart Rustow, *Oil Imports and the National Interest* (New York: Petroleum Industry Research Foundation, March 1971), pp. 3–15.

Western Europe, which has been turning more and more from coal to oil, now relies on the latter for more than half of its energy requirements. Over the last decade it has relied almost entirely on imported oil, and about 85 per cent of those imports have come from the Middle East and North Africa. The volume of imported Middle East oil more than doubled in the 1960s (119.7 million metric tons in 1959 to 274.4 million in 1969) though in percentage it declined from 83 to 53 per cent—this because the percentage of imports from North Africa quadrupled. In projecting current trends, demand will double again by 1980, probably without much change in the 85 per cent share from the combined area.

Japan, with no oil production of its own and rapidly increasing requirements, takes 90 per cent of its imported oil from the Middle East. Japan may attempt to lessen its dependence by developing sources in the Far East, but it is doubtful if such imports can make much of a cut in that percentage.

The economics of the situation leads to some clear conclusions. Without major efforts to raise its present proven reserves or to provide substitutes, in ten years the United States will depend to a substantial extent on imported oil from the Middle East and North Africa. Western Europe and Japan will continue to be highly vulnerable to any interruption of production in the local countries, or of transport from there to the points of consumption. They must therefore be concerned over any threat to continued access to the oil. Such threats could come from another power or from the producing countries themselves.

POSSIBLE THREATS TO SECURITY OF ACCESS

The Soviet Union

The Soviet Union is the only power which might have the capability of interfering with the flow of Middle East oil to Western Europe and Japan, and also a possible interest in exercising that capability. China, whatever the potential of its reserves, can hardly be a factor in the oil trade or oil politics of this decade.

The Soviets have no great need for Middle East oil for their own needs. Soviet reserves in oil and gas are large enough to meet domestic demand for ten years and beyond. Western Siberia has known potential for great expansion. The newly discovered oil in eastern Siberia will be expensive to produce and transport, but the Soviets can exploit it if they wish to give it the necessary priority.[43] They may well have an interest, however, in importing fuel from the Middle East and North Africa, as they are already doing to a small extent, because it can be relatively cheap and also useful for sales to Eastern Europe as well as for earning hard currency and promoting their political purposes elsewhere. Some Eastern European countries, presumably without Soviet objection, are already importing oil directly from Iran and Arab countries.

What of Soviet interest in denying Middle East oil to the West? Can the Soviets get their hands on the faucet, turn it off or on as they like, and thus gain the power of life or death over Europe? This is the specter which has haunted many in the West and has been thought of as a major reason for building a regional security system linking the Middle Eastern countries with the Western powers. How would the Soviet Union acquire control of the producing wells or the routes of transport? It might do so by seizure or by arrangements with the governments of producing countries.

In looking at the record of Soviet policy in the Middle East over the years, it is difficult to see as a real possibility a resort to force to take over oil-producing territory and facilities. Political and military pressure to get a concession in Iran did not work in the 1940s. Seizure of Middle East oil means in effect seizure of the countries which produce it, a major act of aggression which could precipitate a world war. Even if the Soviet Union invaded and took over a major producing country, Iran for example, and were successful in avoiding a wider war, it is questionable whether it could take over the oil wells intact, keep them functioning, and find sufficient markets to provide Iran with the equivalent of its former income. Western companies and consumers would turn to other sources and, without oil income from them, Iran's economy would sink to a lower level, leaving the occupying power with big problems and practically no offsetting benefits.

43. It is difficult to estimate proven reserves in the Soviet Union in comparison with other countries where more information is available (Robert W. Campbell, *The Economics of Soviet Oil and Gas*, Baltimore: The Johns Hopkins Press, 1968, pp. 68–72). The U.N. figure for 1969 is 8 billion tons (*Statistical Yearbook, 1970*, p. 213). Some observers maintain that Soviet reserves are "inadequate" in the sense that much of the crude oil would be far too costly to bring into production (see "Russian Reserves are Inadequate," *Petroleum Press Service*, April 1969, pp. 122–23).

The more likely possibility is a gradual rapprochement between Moscow and the governments of the oil-producing states by which Soviet influence can be exerted on their policies. The pattern might look something like this: growth of national oil companies in the individual producing states as the latter cut down the concessions and established positions of the Western oil companies; Soviet technical aid to those national companies in exploration and production, with repayment to the Soviet Union largely in oil products;[44] Soviet purchase of oil from the national companies to sell in Eastern Europe or other parts of the world; Soviet stimulation of friction between the local governments and the Western oil companies, using the theme of freedom from imperialist exploitation; growing Soviet influence on the policies of those governments to the point where the oil imports of Western Europe and Japan could be adversely affected by Soviet pressure.

Some parts of this general configuration already exist or will shortly come into being. National oil companies will be favored by governments and will expand their share of production. This holds true in Iran, Iraq, Syria, Egypt, and Algeria; it is less evident in more traditionally governed states such as Saudi Arabia, Kuwait, or the sheikhdoms of the Persian Gulf. The situation in itself does not give the Soviet Union a strong or determining influence over the flow of oil to what have been its natural and historic markets. Yet the trend might go further. The Soviets might take for themselves more Middle East oil, deferring expensive exploitation of their own reserves, although they are wary of creating any real degree of dependence on vulnerable sources of supply. They might help producing countries to find alternative markets to Western Europe or Japan, or try to induce them to regulate the terms of sale and delivery of oil as a pressure on Europeans and Japanese to change their policies to conform to interests and ambitions supposedly shared by the Soviets and the local regimes. The extreme case would be a political collaboration so close as to place the actual power of decision in Soviet hands.

These disturbing possibilities, however, posit a situation in which the Soviet Union virtually dominates the oil-producing countries. Is this likely to be the case? Since Stalin's day we have had little evidence of a Soviet determination to turn any Middle Eastern state into a true satellite, or of the willingness of any state in the area to accept that status. Such inroads as Moscow has made have been based on bargains with individual governments by which the latter sought Soviet cooperation to gain objectives of their own. They took Soviet aid, but they did not hand over control of their own resources or of their own governmental decisions. Governments whose plans for national development depend on oil royalties and revenues in hard currency would not permit that income to be reduced or put in jeopardy for the sake of Soviet strategy against the West. Unless, of course, the Soviets could somehow buy oil and extend funds equivalent to that income—an unlikely contingency.

The prospect is quite different, and it will be determined by economics, not by common views on Western imperialism or even on the Arab-Israel dispute. The biggest producers in the Gulf area are involved only indirectly (Saudi Arabia, Kuwait) or not at all (Iran) in that dispute, and even militant Iraq and Libya, when they strike at the West through its oil interests, do so for their own national reasons and not for the benefit of Moscow. We should not over-argue the point. Soviet interests may well be served by the oil policies of national governments which, for whatever reasons, restrict the flow of oil to Western Europe or Japan or make it difficult for the international oil companies to function effectively. Soviet involvement may contribute to the growing feeling of independence from the West already evident in the producing states. But the Soviet hand alone will not be on the faucet.

Producing Countries

It is in the policies of local governments that the more real threats to Western interests, immediate and longer-term, appear to lie. This has long been a worrisome problem, ever since the crisis of 1956 dramatized the vulnerability of Western Europe. That instance was a clear case of political decisions and acts of force which blocked the normal routes of transport (the Suez Canal and the pipelines from the Gulf states to the Mediterranean). It was overcome by emergency measures and by the reasonably rapid restoration of the old routes. The Canal

> 44. In 1966 the U.S.S.R. and Iran concluded a barter agreement covering Soviet aid to industrial projects, including a gas pipeline, in exchange for supplies of natural gas. In 1967 the U.S.S.R. agreed to provide aid to the Iraq National Oil Company in return for payment in oil. Under later agreements, this bargain was extended to cover the rich North Rumaila and Ratawi fields. In March 1972 Moscow announced an agreement with Libya to provide aid for exploration and production of oil and gas.

was open again by the middle of 1957. The Western governments and the oil companies had had a scare, but not one so bad as to induce an all-out effort during the ensuing decade to reduce their condition of dependence by developing alternative sources of oil or other fuels, expanding storage facilities, or subsidizing the rapid building of an emergency fleet of tankers.

When the Arab-Israel dispute exploded in 1967, the Suez Canal was again closed by becoming the front line between two hostile armies, and the vulnerability of the pipelines from the Gulf area to the Mediterranean was again demonstrated. The principal Arab oil-producing countries (Saudi Arabia, Kuwait, Iraq) declared they would not ship oil from their territory to the United States or Britain. These events, however, did not have at the time a devastating effect on Western Europe's oil supplies, although they became tighter and more costly. The closure of the Suez Canal forced Western Europe to get its oil by the much longer Cape route, but the increasing availability of giant tankers helped to reduce the difference in cost. While occasional disruption of the flow of oil through the pipelines to the Mediterranean caused inconvenience and economic loss, here again the big tankers provided a substitute means of transport. West-of-Suez oil, from Libya and Algeria, was available in increasing volume. Finally, the ban on the shipment of Saudi Arabian and Kuwaiti oil to Britain, never really effective because oil sent to other destinations could not be prevented from eventually reaching British ports, was lifted after the Arab conference at Khartoum in August 1967, at which those two countries and Libya agreed to compensate Egypt at the rate of $266 million per year for the loss of Suez Canal revenue. Nevertheless, the basic conditions of dependence, vividly demonstrated by the crisis, remained.

It seems to be a lesson of the period since the war of 1967 that Arab political antagonism toward the West, despite strong rhetoric, is not decisive in its effect on the production and transport of oil. It may be that the relative coolness of European governments toward Israel and their obvious desire to improve relations with the Arab states has had something to do with the latter's moderation. Libya's Premier Qaddafi, however, could not resist nationalizing British Petroleum when Britain let Iran seize some Arab islands in the Persian Gulf at the end of 1971. American interests may be more vulnerable. President Sadat has spoken of striking at American oil interests in retaliation for the delivery of American arms to Israel, but apparently he expects other Arab states to do the striking.

46

The developments of the last few years, and especially of the year 1971, indicate that the real challenge to Western oil interests by the producing countries is not a result of political emotion or spite at a time of crisis. Now led not by wild men but by the Shah and by Sheikh Yamani of Saudi Arabia, it represents a well-calculated economic policy which fits into a long trend, the trend toward greater economic benefits for the governments and the nations which happen to have the oil resources in their territory, especially as they acquire the proficiency to operate and manage things themselves. The motivation is nationalist, anti-imperialist, anti-Western if you like—political in that sense—but the real aim is to exploit bargaining power to gain a greater share in the returns from enormously rich resources. It is in the world-wide pattern of what eventually happens to extractive industries owned by foreign companies in less developed countries. Significantly, the members of the Organization of Petroleum Exporting Countries (OPEC), which prepared the way for this challenge, include Iran, Venezuela, and Indonesia, not just Arabs conditioned by a long anti-Western struggle and by hatred of Israel.

The pressure that has been and may be generated as the local governments and political movements push further in the directions already set will undoubtedly affect the established arrangements by which the Western companies have played the key role in the production, transport, refining, and marketing of Middle Eastern and North African oil. The main questions of a policy nature concern whether and how the vital interests of the consuming nations in access to oil will be affected. These questions must now be considered in the light of the negotiations of 1971 which led to new agreements between the companies and the governments of the producing countries.

THE NEGOTIATIONS OF 1971

There was an inevitability about the push of the producing countries for greater returns and for participation in oil operations. Before 1970 they were held back by the glut of oil on the world market, but in the course of 1970 it became evident that a strong seller's market was developing, the result of (a) an unexpectedly rapid rise in demand, especially in Europe; (b) an interruption of the flow from Saudi Arabia through Tapline to the Mediterranean; and (c) a tanker shortage on the Cape route, pushing freight rates sky-high. Western Europe naturally had increased its imports from Libya, where the transport was easy and relatively cheap, with the result that Libyan oil accounted for about 30 per cent of European requirements.[45] The new revolutionary Libyan regime, seeing its opportunities, began to restrict exports and to demand higher prices. Starting with one small independent company, which capitulated, the Libyans soon were signing agreements with all the concessionaires that included increases in posted prices and in the percentage of Libya's tax take, to about 55 per cent, as an adjustment for past claims.[46]

The Libyan negotiations immediately brought other producing countries to the point of demanding negotiations with the companies under the threat of cutting production down or off. The companies then decided that they would have to negotiate as a group, in order not to be plucked one by one, and the producing countries decided to negotiate on a regional group basis, first the states of the Persian Gulf (principally Iran, Iraq, Kuwait, Saudi Arabia, Abu Dhabi), and then the states delivering oil at Mediterranean ports (Libya again, plus Iraq and Saudi Arabia for their oil coming by pipeline). The Teheran settlement with the Gulf states included higher posted prices right away, plus increases to follow periodically, plus a jump to 55 per cent as the basic income tax rate.

Then it was Libya's turn again to squeeze the companies for another 5 per cent in the tax rate and also for higher prices to take account of the shorter haul to Europe and the low-sulphur content of Libyan oil. Iraq and Saudi Arabia also got satisfaction on the price arrangements for their Mediterranean oil. Nigeria signed comparable agreements; Venezuela had already raised its tax rate to a flat 60 per cent; and Algeria was taking over control of the French concession in that country.

All in all, the companies contracted to pay a large bill as a result of the various settlements. The producing countries figured to gain $3 billion more in 1971 than they would have under the old agreements, and they would be getting an additional $2 billion more per annum by 1975, on the basis of the same volume of oil. The payout, taking into account the expected increase over five years, would be much higher.[47] The ultimate bill, of course, would be paid by the consumers, for the increased costs for the companies would be passed on to them in the form of higher prices.

The settlements of 1971 were made for a five-year period, thus assuring, as company representatives said at the time, a breathing spell in which to carry on normal operations, make adjustments, and plan for the future. Unfortunately, the way in which the storm of 1970–71 had blown up and the stark revelation of the bargaining power of the producing countries, in addition to inevitable political changes, raised some doubt about that five-year period of stability. That the Middle East governments would not ignore a new opportunity to put the bite on the companies again was evident when they called for immediate negotiations for higher payments to make up the losses they would suffer as a result of devaluation of the U.S. dollar; and in January 1972 they won an additional 8.49 per cent from the companies. A more serious question for the companies than paying out more money is the OPEC demand for "participation" in the entire process, from production to marketing, being carried on by the international companies. This the companies would find, in the words of the Chairman of Standard Oil of New Jersey, "extremely difficult to implement."[48] But the acceptance "in principle" by ARAMCO (the operating company in Saudi Arabia owned by four major American companies including Jersey) of 20 per cent participation by the Saudi government opened the way to similar agreements elsewhere, even though the detailed agreements might still be far off. For the producing countries the formula is simple: After cash must come control.[49]

This is the background, and this therefore is the proper time for considering how the advanced nations which depend on Middle East–North African oil can best protect their interest in access to it on tolerable terms. The problem includes not only the producing countries and the oil companies, but the governments of those countries which consume the oil and of those which the companies call home.

PRODUCING COUNTRIES AND FOREIGN OIL COMPANIES

For many years the big international oil companies (mainly American and British but with some French and Dutch participation) have been

45. Walter J. Levy, "Oil Power," *Foreign Affairs*, July 1971, p. 654.
46. J. E. Hartshorn, "From Tripoli to Teheran and Back: The Size and Meaning of the Oil Game," *The World Today*, July 1971, pp. 293–94.
47. Hartshorn, cited, p. 296; Levy, cited, p. 656.
48. *The Wall Street Journal*, November 5, 1971.
49. Peregrine Fellowes, "Living Dangerously—Can Europe Afford to Rely on Middle East Oil?" *New Middle East*, October 1971, p. 26; Michael Field, "Oil: OPEC and Participation," *The World Today*, January 1972, pp. 5–13.

able to operate in the Middle East with concessionary arrangements which brought large profits to the companies and large royalties and revenues to the local governments. In general, the companies were able to stay ahead of the rising pressures and demands of nationalism by instituting the 50-50 pattern on sharing profits, by providing jobs and training to local nationals, and by contributing to the local economy. The one major attempt at nationalization, that of Iran in 1951–53, was defeated because the companies were able to raise production in other countries, and then when Mosaddeq was overthrown, come back to Iran as an international consortium instead of a single British company.

In dealing with individual countries separately the companies had strong bargaining power. It was only when the producing countries began to sense the strength of their position—as the Shah of Iran did in his annual tug of war with the consortium over production levels and prices, and as the military junta in Libya did in choosing the right moment to pick off the companies one by one—that the balance of bargaining power began to shift. The device by which governments of varying complexion, Arab and non-Arab, came together this past year put the companies into a position where even their counterdevice of negotiating as a unit could not prevent a settlement more or less on the producing countries' terms.

The main questions now are how far those countries will try to push their luck, whether the companies will stay in business and on what terms, and what alternatives can be found if the present arrangements should break down. The profit margins of the companies have narrowed to the point where they say they are barely in line with competitive rates in other industries; pressure on them for a bigger "take" can only be satisfied by higher world prices, and that is indeed what happened after the agreements of 1971.[50]

As the prospects look, the producing countries are going to have their superior bargaining position for several years anyway. They can press for higher prices, squeeze out higher taxes, manipulate production up or down, and demand participation in ownership both for production and for downstream operations. But they will not gain by pushing beyond that point where production, transport, refining, or marketing are adversely affected. The time for adjustments satisfactory to both parties may be fairly short.

The companies still have a number of means at their disposal to avoid being pushed to the wall, especially their control of the networks for global distribution of oil and their capital for further exploration and development. Yet they may be forced out of the production business by acts of nationalization or by demands they cannot meet. Contractual relationships may replace the existing concessions. Or the companies could perhaps change their role to that of buyers of crude or petroleum products at the producing countries' ports, whence they would transport and market them as they do now, although this arrangement would not be attractive without an assured source of supply. Recent purchase agreements with Algeria's national company may point the way.[51]

If the companies were forced to the wall, then the question would be whether the various national and nationalized companies run by the local governments could produce and deliver enough oil to satisfy both themselves and the consumers in Europe, Japan, and elsewhere. They would not find it easy to do so, at least not for quite a number of years, although the consuming countries would feel the need for drastic measures to make sure oil was available. The Shah of Iran, in letting it be known that he intends to terminate the contract with the international consortium in 1979, and the government of Venezuela, in confirming the reversion of foreign concessions starting in 1983, have indicated what they think is the time needed to prepare for full takeover; it might come before then, but hardly later. They are two of the most advanced countries, better able to handle production on their own, but others are not likely to hold back once the wind starts blowing strongly in that direction. For the Arab countries, Algeria, which has just taken over majority control of the French companies operating there, may be the model rather than Iran or Venezuela.

In the Algerian case, the terms set by the government in February 1971 were unacceptable to the French, particularly the low figure for compensation, the demand for back taxes, and the limitation of future access to Algerian oil. After months of negotiation marked by great strain, during which France boycotted Algerian oil and tried without success to get other countries to do the same, the respective French

50. Levy, cited, p. 657.
51. In late 1970, Mobil and Royal Dutch announced large-scale purchase agreements for Algerian crude following settlements on the expropriation of their properties. At the beginning of 1972, Standard Oil (New Jersey) made a deal for $400 million worth of Algerian oil to be delivered over a 4-year period (see *The Wall Street Journal*, January 5, 1972).

companies reached agreement with the Algerian national company later in the year.[52] The salient facts were that the takeover of control of the French companies was accepted and that France's "special position" was gone. France will undoubtedly continue as a major importer of Algerian oil, but all foreign companies (including American) will now be there on an equal basis, and on Algeria's terms.

What we are likely to see in the area over the next decade is a mixed situation in which the major companies are still operating but under the pressure of increasing demands; the local governments are building up and favoring their own national oil companies; contractual agreements for technical cooperation and for sales are being made by these national companies with independent Western companies, with government-controlled organizations in consuming countries, and with agencies of communist governments. Increasingly the producing countries will try to get into downstream operations either by insisting on participation in those of the major companies, or by building their own refineries and tanker fleets with such outside help as they can get.

Compared to the relatively stable situation of the past two decades, this entire picture looks to be one of confusion, altercation, and disruption of established practices which have rather effectively served the interests of producing countries, consuming countries, and, without any doubt, the big oil companies and their own "mother countries." We can predict that the governments of producing countries will keep on the pressure, and that the international oil companies will try to stay in business in the Middle East as long as they can. But what about the third party, the consumers?

INTERESTS OF THE CONSUMING COUNTRIES

The consuming countries of Western Europe are not represented evenly (and most not at all) in the major international companies operating in the Middle East and North Africa. As the U.S. participation in the Middle East is over 50 per cent (and in Libya about 85 per cent), European interests share only the remainder, in which Britain is the major participant and French interests account for about 6 per cent. These facts necessarily color the views of the others.

Great Britain

Britain has been closely connected with Middle East oil in a triple role: as home of two of the major internationals, as a major consumer itself, and as the place the rulers of some of the richer producing countries have chosen to invest their oil earnings.

The British are there by history and tradition, having been the original Westerners operating in the area, first in Iran and afterwards in Iraq and the Persian Gulf. Even before the Second World War, American companies came increasingly onto the scene, and after the war they gained the largest share; but British interests remained greater in Iraq, shared the concession in Kuwait 50-50 with an American company, and regained a place in Iran after the nationalization crisis of the early 1950s as a partner in the new international consortium. Britain has been heavily involved as financial beneficiary in the production and sales end of the business through British Petroleum (in which the government has a controlling interest) and Shell.[53] On a net basis (less reinvested earnings) the contribution by British oil companies to the country's payments position is an estimated half billion dollars a year, to which the deposits of Middle Eastern rulers add about another half billion.

More recently, as the position of coal in the economy has declined, Great Britain has had to be very much concerned with its position as oil consumer. Consumption more than doubled in the past decade, and in 1970 was second in Western Europe only to that of West Germany. While the Suez crisis of 1956 was resolved before it had any substantial effect on the consumer—although shipments to Britain were cut off for a short while and America, for political reasons, was not helpful in seeing that Western Hemisphere oil was made available— it nonetheless raised the British government's fears of a possible future energy gap. The 1967 crisis, which produced another embargo by Arab countries, heightened this concern although it too was resolved before supplies were jeopardized. New oil sources in the North Sea, which the British expect to go a long way toward alleviating their dependence

52. Agreement was reached with the Compagnie Française des Pétroles (C.F.P.) on June 30, and with the governmental Enterprise des Recherches et d'Activités Pétrolières (ERAP) on December 15, 1971.

53. For the details of ownership of British Petroleum and Royal Dutch-Shell, see Edith T. Penrose, *The Large International Firm in Developing Countries: The International Petroleum Industry* (London: George Allen and Unwin, 1968), pp. 101-16.

on the Middle East, will not provide an answer in the next few years.

A major question arising from Britain's various interests in Middle East oil is the possible conflict in its dual role as a consumer and as the home of two major oil companies. The official assumption has been that the interests of the government and of the companies coincide, but contradictions may be sharpened as Britain moves into the E.E.C. The common interest with its partners as a consumer is clear enough. But will the British accommodate themselves to continental views on the operations of the major international companies? If their own policy is clear, they may be in an excellent position to help reconcile differences between Europe and the United States.

France

President de Gaulle's policy for France has been summed up in the phrase, "oil is independence." Dissatisfied that France had only a minor share in the big Middle East concessions, and wishing to avoid dependence on supplies from "Anglo-Saxon" oil companies, he sought to insulate his country from the world market by increasing the proportion of imports supplied by French companies. France's governmental oil enterprise, ERAP, concluded some special agreements with Saudi Arabia, Iran and Iraq. These moves have been part of a general policy including economic and cultural agreements, as well as offers to supply arms, with those Gulf states which up to the closure of the Suez Canal in 1967 provided France with half its oil needs.

The prize exhibit of French policy was the arrangement with Algeria, reached in 1965, by which French companies held a privileged position in the Algerian oil industry—to match France's "special relationship" in the political and cultural realms—and that country's oil exports went largely to France at fixed prices. But unfortunately for the French policy of independence, the Algerian policy of independence swept most of it away in 1971. For all their show of a national policy, the French companies were only too glad to join the negotiating team which bargained with the producing countries at Teheran and Tripoli.

More recently the French Energy Commission, in pointing out that 70 per cent of France's energy needs will be supplied by oil over the next fifteen years and that the country is becoming increasingly dependent on external energy sources, emphasized the need for diversified sources of oil (particularly outside the Middle East–North African area), greatly increased storage capacity, and a larger tanker fleet, as well as more rapid development of nuclear power at home.[54] Nationalism is the inspiration for such a program. But will any European country be able to afford this type of independence in the conditions of the 1970s?

Italy

Italy too has had a policy of reducing dependence on the primarily American and British major companies and escaping what is seen as subjugation to their high-price system. Toward this end it has made separate deals—giving more favorable terms than offered by the internationals—with producing countries. The Italian state-owned Ente Nazionale Idrocarburi (E.N.I.) was one of the first of the "newcomers" to challenge the majors by offering better terms to producing countries. By its deal with Iran, for example, E.N.I. agreed to carry the exploratory costs and, if oil were found, to split the profits with the National Iranian Oil Company on what was in effect a 25–75 arrangement when the big companies in the international consortium were on a 50–50 basis.

Italy also tried to show its independence, and to get cheaper oil, by imports from the Soviet Union, a policy formalized in a large-scale bilateral trade agreement signed by the two countries in 1963. During most of the 1960s, Italy took up to 15 per cent of its crude oil imports from the U.S.S.R., but that percentage has dropped as Italy's total demand has risen and less Soviet oil has been available for export.

Experience with these policies has not been crowned with much success. The Italians have found no real alternative to filling their growing needs for oil through the big companies. But they definitely feel restive under a system where basic decisions are made without their participation. Hence their growing support for the idea of a European energy policy in which Italy would share. It fits in with the idea that there must be a European policy, in which Italy can play an important part, for economic cooperation and development in the whole Mediterranean area.[55].

54. *Petroleum Press Service*, August 1971, pp. 294–97.

55. Nino Kucich, "Il problema europeo di una politica energetica," *Affari Esteri*, October 1971, pp. 112–26. On the broader approach, see Cesare Merlini, "Italy's International Position: Opportunities and Temptations," *Lo Spettatore Internazionale*, July-August 1971, pp. 264–70.

The Federal Republic of Germany

West Germany, concerned with the extent to which foreign companies have come to dominate its own market, has had the same general ideas as France and Italy on the need for a national policy. It has fostered a national oil organization (Deminex), representing a group of German companies, to engage in trade and to negotiate agreements with foreign governments. The German government in the past largely left international oil matters up to the major international companies and those Western nations more traditionally involved in the Middle East but, after the shock of the negotiations of 1971, has let it be known that this will no longer be the case.

For the Federal Republic, an expansion of all kinds of trade with and aid to the Middle East is linked to the assumption of a more active national policy on oil. German companies are becoming directly involved in producing countries through links with the big internationals. Perhaps more significant, the Federal Republic in March 1972 entered into an agreement with Iran involving not only large-scale oil purchases but also the establishment of a joint company to deal with both production and distribution. In addition, the German desire to resume relations with the Arab countries, broken by them in 1965, can be linked with its desire to assure its oil supplies. But Bonn is also looking farther afield. In the wake of the 1971 developments, it began to show new interest in seeking Latin American sources.[56]

Japan

In the early 1950s Japan began to expand its oil imports to meet its energy needs.[57] The oil had to come from the Middle East in steadily increasing volume; and, as Japan's demands increased through the 1960s, the Middle East's share of its total oil imports reached a plateau at 90 per cent. Because most of that oil came through the big international companies, the Japanese were concerned over its high cost in foreign exchange.

One protective device was to negotiate Middle East concessions for their own producing companies, and this they did in the Saudi-Kuwait Neutral Zone, Abu Dhabi, and Qatar. These companies, which from the start gave the local governments a larger cut than the Western companies did, have not run afoul of political animosity and have not been under as much nationalist pressure. Other devices were to build up their own refineries and to develop a petrochemical industry, in order to cut the cost of refined products. The Japanese government retained wide control over all activities of the industry at home and also subsidized development of new sources of oil and gas both at home and abroad. Japanese companies, with governmental aid, bought interests in a number of enterprises in Alaska, Canada, Indonesia, Australia and elsewhere, and are considering with the U.S.S.R. joint projects for development of oil and gas in eastern Siberia, much of which would flow to Japan.

Despite all this effort, the dream of low-cost, secure supplies provided by fully integrated Japanese companies has not materialized. Even the petroleum plan adopted in 1967 set a goal no higher than 30 per cent for the Japanese-contributed share of total oil demand by 1985.[58] There seems no easy escape for Japan, any more than for France or Italy, in the shape of an independent national policy for oil or for energy as a whole.

The oil settlements reached in 1971 have had their most chastening effect on the consuming countries, for the prices they pay for oil have been raised to meet the companies' expanded obligations to the producing countries. Walter Levy estimates Western Europe's added cost between 1970 and 1975 at as much as $5.5 billion, and Japan's at over $1.5 billion.[59] That is a severe financial blow, in that it means paying out more in foreign exchange and probably reducing the amount of taxation the governments can load onto their own local consumers. As Japan already has, the Western European governments are looking more sharply than before at the whole system by which they get their oil, both as to reliability of supply and as to cost.

Up to now those governments have been rather slow to assert their interests. They have long held to the idea that Middle East oil is vital to them. That idea was partially responsible for the strong British and French reaction to Abdel Nasser's seizure of the Suez Canal Company in 1956, and for Britain's retention for years after the Suez fiasco of military positions at Aden and in the Gulf. When the realization came

56. *U.S. News and World Report*, April 19, 1971.
57. See Peter R. Odell, *Oil and World Politics: A Geographical Interpretation* (New York: Taplinger, 1970), pp. 117–29; and Sevinc Carlson, "Japan's Inroads into the Middle East and North Africa," *New Middle East*, July 1970, pp. 14–17, for background information on Japan's activities relating to Middle East oil.
58. Odell, cited, p. 126–28.
59. Levy, cited, p. 656.

that military measures were neither an economic nor an effective way to guarantee the continued supply of oil, the Western European governments were already aware that they had to pay heed to the susceptibilities of the Middle Eastern nations in order not to jeopardize it. Indeed, West Germany and other consuming countries had no reason to thank Britain and France for undertaking the policies that brought on the closure of the Suez Canal in 1956, or to be patient with the effects of the Arab-Israel deadlock on the security and continuity of oil supplies.

For the Western European governments, after the shock of the major companies' surrender in the negotiations of 1971, the question remains whether they should continue to leave all such matters to the companies or move deliberately toward direct dealings with the producing countries. The Europeans may blame the companies for getting into a position of having to bargain without much bargaining power. But that situation developed, especially in Libya, without either the companies or the consuming countries foreseeing its consequences.

If the prediction that a mixed situation full of uncertainty lies ahead in the next decade is correct, we can expect more active policies on the part of the consuming countries to safeguard their own interests. That will mean a new look by European governments at the ability of the major companies to deliver oil products at acceptable prices, and presumably closer consultation with the companies to advance the interests of both, but not automatic support and diplomatic backing for the companies' policies. They may wish to keep the companies in their present economic role but not leave in their hands the whole responsibility for negotiation with the producing countries. With the latter, the consuming countries will want closer relations to see where attention to political issues may improve the prospects on oil and to explore the possibilities of trade, technical assistance, and other means of cooperation.

If the position of the companies grows weak or untenable, the Western European governments will undoubtedly look at what the producing countries themselves may offer directly. As the producing countries try to go downstream, the consuming countries will try to go upstream, and both trends impinge on the territory of the companies. Finally, we may expect a more prickly attitude in the consuming countries toward the dominant position of the international companies in their own national markets; in other words, the companies may be contending with local nationalism at the lower as well as the upper end of the oil stream.[60]

The Western European countries are hardly likely to develop effective policies if each one tries to do so on its own. The common interest in access to oil at acceptable cost is common to all, and it looms larger than any advantage to be anticipated by specific deals engineered by one to the exclusion of others. The institutional framework for discussion and establishment of a common policy for the main consumers is already at hand: the European Economic Community, whose officials have already begun to discuss the main elements of a European program.[61] When the Six become Ten, all but a few of the European consumer countries will be in it.

For the past several years E.E.C. committees have been suggesting a common approach toward an assured supply of energy by development of local European sources, acquisition of new overseas sources of crude oil, coordinated policies on imports, and steps to enable European oil companies to meet the competition of the giant internationals. These proposals, however, are still little more than proposals. One reason has been concentration on national concerns, with each country scrambling for advantage to itself. The French thought they would control the Sahara wells forever; the Germans, who were the most vulnerable, did not feel the need to question the existing pattern; only the Italians pushed for common action. Another reason has been the complacent and nearly universal belief that in any situation short of total war the oil of the Middle East and North Africa will remain available to Western Europe. That belief may be well founded, but it scarcely justifies a neglect of policies that can help to make it so.

In some respects the O.E.C.D. provides a better forum than the E.E.C. because it includes the United States, Canada, and Japan in addition to a wider European representation. It has been helpful in emergencies and has carried out useful studies. Which institution is used depends on the purpose. The O.E.C.D. is the right place to reconcile differing interests in production, consumption, and the commercial and financial aspects of both, although its members have not been willing to make much use of it. The E.E.C., on the other hand, is the place to

60. Jean-Jacques Berreby, "The Oil Companies' Double Game," *New Middle East*, March 1971, pp. 22–24, represents an example of this line of thought.

61. W. G. Jensen, *Energy and the Economy of Nations* (Henley-on-Thames: G. T. Foulis, 1970), pp. 152–57.

work out policies for Europe. Because it is already a powerful economic unit, able to act as such in international economic affairs, it has a potential for giving Europe real bargaining power. If Europe cannot live without Middle East and North African oil, neither can the producing countries live in the manner to which they have become accustomed without the European market.

WHAT COMMON GROUND?

By way of summary the main conclusions can be briefly put:

1. It is a vital interest of Western Europe and of Japan to have continued access to the oil of the Middle East and North Africa.
2. The United States is not now similarly situated so far as its own supply is concerned, but is likely to become more and more dependent on oil from that region in the future; meanwhile, it has a strong interest in continued access on the part of Western Europe and Japan, its principal allies.
3. The Soviet Union and China, although they may enter the oil picture in the Middle East and North Africa, will not play a dominant or major part because they cannot provide the producing countries with alternative transport systems or markets for the bulk of their oil.
4. Consequently, the future patterns in the oil industry and trade will be determined largely by the relationships among three main parties: the producing countries, the major international oil companies, and the consuming countries.
5. Because the overriding interest, for all the advanced nations, is the continued availability of oil to the main consuming countries, the governments of the latter should have the leading role in preserving that interest; the commercial and financial interests of the companies and of their home countries are important but subordinate to the overriding interest in continued access.
6. The bargaining power of the advanced nations in dealing with the Middle Eastern and North African governments is most likely to be maintained and enhanced if it is backed by (a) expanding political and economic relations which benefit the producing countries, and (b) the development of alternative sources of energy outside the Middle East–North African region.

The task of moving from these general propositions to actual policies requires both a division of labor and a willingness to abandon some well-established ideas and practices. Some of the Western powers have been under a considerable handicap in relations with the oil-producing nations, especially the Arab nations, because of the old issues of colonialism and imperialism and because of the Arab-Israel conflict. It is essential to limit the damage resulting from these issues and to put relations with Arab countries on a new basis of cooperation. The economies of the Western European countries are complementary with theirs. Europe is much less vulnerable than the United States on the question of Israel, and Japan is not vulnerable at all. Accordingly, Western Europe and Japan should take the lead in trying to build up trade with the oil-producing countries and to assist in their development. The United States should follow the same policy, but it can hardly make much progress until the Arab-Israel conflict moves to a more settled stage.

The case of Saudi Arabia deserves special mention. It has the largest oil reserves of any country in the world and in future years will probably have the largest annual production. It is now the world's leading exporter. The only foreign company there is ARAMCO, and the United States has had an especially close relationship with the Saudi government. It is important to maintain contractual and political relationships which are useful to all concerned. It is important, as well, to remember that the primary interest in Saudi Arabian oil is its availability to all the advanced noncommunist nations. And Saudi Arabia's policies and politics are not immune to change. The major continuing interest of the West is to determine how, in the evolving overall relationship with that country and its neighbors, access to oil can best be met over the long term. It is a broad world problem which should not rest on a restricted base from either the producers' or the consumers' side.

Two crucial requirements—meeting unexpected crises in supply and finding long-term alternative sources—may be the ultimate defense which cannot be permitted to fail. The immediate European needs for stored supplies adequate for six months or more and for tanker tonnage sufficient to cope with disruption of transport routes have been foreseen, but not wholly met because they require subsidies. All the concerned nations must be ready again, if Europe is cut off from needed Middle East supplies, to fill part of the gap with oil from the Western Hemisphere—it could not be totally filled even with rationing in Europe and the United States. As to the long-term needs for energy, major new prospects for oil and gas must be sought and developed, both for their own sake and to increase bargaining power in the Middle East and North Africa.

Central to the problems of the future are the respective roles to be played by governments and by the three different types of oil companies: the big internationals, most of them American, which have tended to dominate the noncommunist world's oil business from producing well to service station and whose decisions and negotiations with governments affect the lifeblood of national economies; the companies of the main consuming nations which are, for the most part, governmental agencies carrying out national policies; and the "independents," smaller private companies engaged in one or another aspect of the international oil business and less able than their big rivals to afford the long political view. The need for coordination of policy to serve the interests of all the advanced nations requires a much firmer understanding among governments and companies on what is to be done and who is to do it.

The theory under which the major companies automatically serve the interests of all by pursuing their own—that their worldwide operations are more efficient than any others could be, and that they are a useful buffer between governments of producing and consuming countries thus helping to keep oil out of international politics—has been held not only by the companies themselves but generally by many governments as well. Without them, the world oil industry would not have had its spectacular development. Yet the increasing pressure on the companies, especially the way in which they have had to retreat before the demands of the OPEC group, has raised questions about how well the theory is working.

How can the respective governments and the various types of companies bring their perceived interests and their activities into greater harmony. The President of Continental Oil has called for the marshalling of "massive countervailing power" to check the power shown by the producing countries acting together, to be exercised mainly by the companies within "a strong framework for collective action at the top diplomatic levels on behalf of the consuming nations."[62] Whether or not massive governmental support for the companies in a showdown with Middle East governments is the panacea, the time has surely come for a determination of long-range policy by governments in which the questions of how to deal with the oil politics of the Middle East and North Africa, what the role of private and governmental companies should be, and how the costs may be met, find their place in overall policies on fuel and energy.

IV.

THE ADVANCED NATIONS: CONCERTED OR SEPARATE POLICIES?

How do all parts of the problem fit together, if they do? Do the United States, the nations of Western Europe, and Japan have real conflicts of interest or merely different ways of looking at interests which they share? In either case they should consider how they may benefit by joint or parallel action or by separate and different policies.

Looking at the whole problem of security in the Mediterranean–Middle East–Indian Ocean region, the Western nations share three requirements: (1) maintenance of the global deterrent; (2) maintenance of a military balance to Soviet armed forces in the region in order to prevent use of the latter to establish positions of domination at the expense of important Western interests and of the independence of local states; (3) development of political and other relations with local states and with outside powers toward understandings and settlements which in time can replace the military balance as a basis for security.

On the first point, the main responsibility rests with the United States both to maintain the deterrent and to negotiate limitations on the strategic arms race with the Soviet Union, a reality which is recognized by the Western European nations and by Japan. They need not enter into detailed calculations with the United States on how to cope with a general war arising in the Middle East. This is a contingency which both superpowers have strong reasons to avoid. If they allow it to happen, it will occur because of their own failure of sanity and statesmanship in handling a local conflict or their relations with each other. All that other nations can do is help to temper or settle disputes which could possibly lead to that result.

The second and third points are related. Under present conditions the Western nations have to decide, singly or in cooperation, what are their minimum needs in military forces and deployments. At the same time they should explore all possibilities of using other than military means to attain the desired results. They need not assume for all time that the only relevant factors for security in the region are the number and location of ships and bases or the definition of security commit-

62. John G. McLean, in *The Oil Daily*, December 29, 1971.

ments. But these things are important now, and the requirements of security pose a practical question: How much is enough?

We need not make the assumption that a Soviet lunge for domination of the Mediterranean, the Indian Ocean, or the land areas surrounding them is likely, or would have much chance of success if it were tried. Yet we must assume that the Russians intend to make the most of the extension of their military reach. They might decide to use their forces to intervene in one country or another, to support a friendly regime or to help overthrow an unfriendly one. These possibilities touch the interests of all the advanced nations: their political standing, their need for freedom of access and communication, and their continued supply of oil.

The main military question for those nations is whether the Soviet buildup of military power should be answered in kind. They cannot force its removal or reduction by ultimatum or direct action. They can perhaps, over time, work on the political situation so that the Soviet military forces are not welcomed by local governments or cease to serve Soviet political purposes. They can attempt to work out with the Soviet Union arrangements for stabilizing or limiting arms levels in the region, or for political settlements which would have the same result. In the absence of any of these positive developments, it is hard to avoid the conclusion that a balance of non-nuclear military power must be maintained as a background for political and diplomatic action. There is no one-to-one correspondence between military power and political influence or advantage. In some cases the psychological effect of the direction in which things are moving, the impression that Soviet power is increasing and that of America going down (even though the latter is still greater in absolute terms), can have significant political consequences. If there is a generally accepted situation of equilibrium, then the erosion of Western interests and the danger of Soviet political primacy in the region may be avoided.

The Mediterranean will not again be an American lake, but neither can it be allowed to become a Russian lake. The U.S. Sixth Fleet, at this juncture, is an indispensable part of the balance; and a marked reduction, such as withdrawal of an aircraft carrier and supporting units, could have adverse political as well as military effects. Perhaps American power in itself is enough to check Soviet power, but it would be better for the general security if elements other than the two superpowers had a significant part in maintaining it. Naval forces of France, Italy, and Great Britain, cooperating under a NATO label so long as

NATO has commitments there, could provide that element. For the future, a European label would be more effective by taking the edge off the strictly bilateral confrontation of the two biggest powers. Such forces would have the possibility of gaining the active or passive cooperation of those of nonaligned countries such as Spain, Yugoslavia, and perhaps even the Arab countries of the Maghreb.

At the present time the idea that both the American and the Soviet fleets should withdraw from the Mediterranean is fanciful. What is important is that other actors appear on the scene, with naval forces and a responsibility for security more proportionate to their real political and economic interests in that area. The presence of European forces, of course, would require some understandings with the United States about purpose and policy. The Europeans are aware of the twofold mission of the Sixth Fleet, which is in the Mediterranean to fulfill NATO obligations but also to uphold American interests in the Middle East that may have little or nothing to do with NATO or Europe. If the United States, for example, wanted to position the Sixth Fleet at some point in the eastern Mediterranean to deter a military move against Israel or Jordan, it could not expect British or Italian or French units to cooperate unless those governments supported the political objective. The military factors, accordingly, ought to push the Western nations toward closer coordination of policy.

Similar considerations apply to the Indian Ocean, although there the strategic factors are more attenuated. The question is again one of balance, in which a minimal Western military presence is necessary to provide a counter to the Soviet. If the Suez Canal is reopened, one can expect that the Soviet presence will expand, requiring some further buildup on the other side. Here too a combination of Western forces, including Australian, is preferable to an assumption of the task by any one of them. Europe's interest is clear because of its interest in oil, although the idea that military power alone can guarantee oil supply has rightly been abandoned. Japan's interest is also apparent, although the time has not come for a Japanese military presence in this region. The purpose of the desired equilibrium is to give scope to peaceful trade and to the political and economic development of the countries of the region without their being affected by military pressure or intervention on the part of any outside power.

On a broader basis, the primacy of the political factor emerges from a review of how the Soviet Union gained its present military position in the Mediterranean. It did so not just by sending in vessels, but by establishing a pattern of military collaboration with certain states which then provided naval and air facilities. The Soviets' relationship with Egypt, which includes de facto naval bases and a number of airfields wholly controlled by Soviet personnel and adds tremendously to their military capabilities, was attained by diplomacy, military and economic aid, and finally, a formal treaty.

Similarly, east of Suez the possession of force is less likely than the use of political positions gained by diplomacy to secure the entrenchment, or the withdrawal, of military power. Thus, the regime in Southern Yemen opens the base at Aden to Soviet use because Soviet policy has generally supported that regime against those it takes to be its enemies. The new Soviet treaty with India may provide the foundation for a military cooperation not unlike that between the U.S.S.R. and Egypt. Ceylon may be receptive to military cooperation with Moscow when it receives Soviet arms to use against domestic enemies. The Soviets, by backing some East African state like Somalia in its local quarrels, may also get a foothold there. Western military power has not prevented such developments in the past and cannot easily do so in the future. But Soviet power, conversely, cannot easily make itself felt in countries where Western diplomacy has been successful.

And so the argument comes back to the point that the security of the advanced nations of the West depends only in a general way on what armed forces they keep on the spot or in readiness to move there. It depends more on the attitudes of local states and on the policies of Western nations affecting those attitudes. There is a necessary minimum of physical presence, certainly, to show that the West is neither impotent nor indifferent. But beyond the military measures necessary to counterbalance Soviet power and to rule out disaster, the main effort must be political. The clearest lessons of recent years are that Western Europe can be more effective in its own interest by developing common policies of its own, and that it can best support the general purposes it shares with America by seeking at the same time both an independent role and a practice of coordination with Washington where a true basis for it can be found. The accent of European policy should be on Europe. In that way the policies of France may lose some of their nationalistic bite and be reconciled with those of its European partners.

No more eloquent European appeal for such a vision has been made than that of Edward Heath, speaking to a German audience before he became Prime Minister and before Britain's decision to enter the E.E.C.:

> The single most important thing to make an impact on public opinion would be if Europe could speak with one voice on an important problem. . . . In the Middle East we all have the same interests. We do not want to see Israel go under. And we all depend on good relations with the Arab countries for the oil vital to our industrial life. We do not want Soviet encroachment in the Mediterranean, nor a clash between the Big Powers. If in Four-Power talks on the Middle East, Britain and France spoke with the weight of a united Europe behind them, much could be achieved. The Common Market must be more than haggling over butter and coal.[63]

Analysis of the Arab-Israel problem also shows that Western Europe has played a role well below the magnitude of its interests in the area. The main European concern, of course, is that no war break out and that the conflict be somehow settled or appeased so that it has a minimum adverse affect on security and on the flow of oil to European markets. Different schools of thought exist on how to bring about that result: Some think that only the two superpowers, each exerting influence on its own clients, can bring about a settlement; some look to the United States, as the only power able to persuade or coerce Israel, to do the trick; others would like to see the parties left alone to make their own terms.

None of these courses, as our earlier discussion has shown, offers great possibilities of success. The nations of Western Europe, accordingly, have to consider what they themselves can do in facing up to an extended period in which no progress is made toward an Arab-Israel settlement. They are frustrated today in the Middle East because they have so little to say, whereas historically and geographically and in basic interests they are very close. One reason for their ineffectiveness is the lack of unity. Great Britain has tended to support American initiatives, while France has sought a role of its own, and Italy and Germany have hung back. Together they could provide both Arabs and Israelis another partner to look to and listen to. The Big-Four concept cherished by General de Gaulle actually provided the British and French with no great influence either on the other two of the Big Four or on the Arab states and Israel.

Their presence, with others, as "Europe," carrying out the intention behind the initial effort of the members of the E.E.C. to work out a

63. Adapted from *The Times*, May 9, 1970, where Heath's remarks are reported in indirect quotation.

policy resting on interests common to all, may be quite a different proposition. Western Europe as a whole, with the power it would have and the opportunities it could offer, represents an economic partner of great importance to both sides, as well as a possible modifier of the rigidities of Soviet and American policies.

Israel, which is engaged in trying to make U.S. policy more rigid than it presently is, will not be attracted by that second point. But as the conflict goes on, Israel may find some greater prospect of security with Europe in the picture than in a total reliance on frontiers supposedly secured by geography and the continuing inflow of American arms to maintain them indefinitely. Should the United States object? Thus far it has not welcomed French attempts to find compromise solutions, but a European rather than a French policy, instead of helping the Soviets, could help cut the ground under their feet in their relations with the Arabs.

The fact of the matter is that there cannot be any compromise or settlement unless Israel is prepared to soften its own rigid policies. Perhaps only the combined influence of the nations of North America and Western Europe, all of them desirous of normal and fruitful relations with Arab states and fundamentally dedicated as well to Israel's right to live in security but unwilling to support present Israeli policies and tactics, can bring the possibility of a settlement to reality. That Arab leaders and governments will have to compromise their extreme positions is also clear. The world community, in the long run, cannot permit small nations in the Middle East to keep the world forever on the edge of war, and neither Israel nor the Arab states can easily contemplate the consequences of persisting indifference or hostility on their part toward the unique community which the economically advanced nations of the West represent.

A deeper perspective on these possibilities may be obtained from the relation of these political and security matters to the ever-present subject of oil. There the analysis leads even more strongly to the conclusion that the advanced nations, especially those of Western Europe, should forge as solid and lasting a relationship as they can with the producing countries. These should be broad relationships encompassing an expansion of exports by the industrially advanced nations, investment, technical assistance, collaboration in development, and also a renewal and expansion of cultural ties which still exist despite years of political struggle. To build up a complex of such relationships is to create mutual interests which can outlast changes of regime and thus minimize the effect of chronic political instability in the Middle East, since any regime would have something to lose by disruption of the framework of collaboration.

The idea that grand schemes of regional economic development will produce the solution to political conflicts has a great attraction, especially for Americans. But there are some lessons in the fate of the Eric Johnston plan for the division and development of the waters of the Jordan River, the idea of Dag Hammarskjöld to find a solution for the Palestine refugee problem in the context of a broad economic advance in the Middle East, and the Eisenhower-Strauss plan for large nuclear desalting plants to make the desert bloom in Israel and in neighboring Arab states and thus bring peace out of conflict. Specific and more modest projects offering concrete mutual economic benefits, such as the planned oil pipeline across Egypt from Suez to Alexandria to be financed by European interests and used for Europe-bound oil, illustrate a sounder way to build up the desired network of cooperation.

The United States and Japan have every reason to support and contribute to the creation of that network. They also have every reason to work together with Western Europe toward a long-range energy policy which will lessen their dependence on the oil of the Middle East and North Africa. Individually, all the advanced nations have been working out their own long-range plans, with emphasis on national security and the undesirability of dependence on outside sources. That has been the main difficulty, since separate national plans become set as they are put into practice and tend to shut off the avenues to international planning and agreement, and competing national plans will not serve any nation well. President Nixon has spoken of the need for a long-range U.S. policy, including coal, oil, gas, and oil-shale, as well as atomic, solar, geothermal, tidal, and other forms of energy.[64] American officials have also thought in terms of North America or the Western Hemisphere, thus one or two stages beyond a national plan; and the E.E.C. has at least talked about a common policy for Western Europe. All these endeavors should go forward but in some rational relation to each other, not only to meet future needs, but to face the crucial question of continued precarious dependence on an unstable and unpredictable Middle East.

> 64. Message to Congress, June 4, 1971 (*Weekly Compilation of Presidential Documents*, June 7, 1971, pp. 855–66). The message is a statement of possibilities rather than an integrated plan.

There is nothing inherently inconsistent between that aim and a policy of broad collaboration with the Middle Eastern countries. It is merely a matter of simple prudence. It is possible, with active and co-ordinated policies on energy, that the critical dependence of the West and of Japan on Middle East oil is a temporary state of affairs that will endure only for some ten to fifteen years until atomic energy (which may supply up to 15 per cent of the industrial nations' needs by 1980) and other sources of power can replace it, and that all we have to do is baby along the producing countries until then. But to look on a broad policy of collaboration between the advanced nations and those of the Middle East and North Africa as a temporary device for the sake of oil alone is to underestimate its importance and its potential. For it can help to ease or to contain political conflicts, to permit rational attack on the area's economic problems, and to create a state of affairs to which the Soviet Union will have to accommodate and might find advantage in so doing.

What of the negative side? What if the advanced nations do not concert their policies? The United States is likely to be left alone with a big and unmanageable military assignment, trying to maneuver among the Israelis, Arabs, and Russians without much chance of success and no easy way out, and questioning the wisdom of trying to protect the interests of others with no help in return from them. The Western European nations, each looking primarily to its own concerns, would tend to shy away from U.S. policies which to them smack more of the cold war and of over-concern with Israel than of common Western interests, but would be unable to replace them with anything better. They might turn to making their own arrangements with the Arab states at the expense of both Israeli and American interests. On oil matters, the probability would be for friction between American oil companies and those of Europe and Japan, and between Washington and its allies. Opportunities for exploitation of these differences by Middle Eastern governments and by the Kremlin would inevitably follow.

The lesson to be drawn from such negative predictions seems clear enough. Yet the developments since August 1971 in relations among the advanced industrial nations scarcely augur well for efforts to apply that lesson in the Middle East. The evidence of shocked sensibilities, mutual ill will, and resurgent nationalism is to be found just about everywhere. It is anyone's guess when the current tensions and controversies over currencies, trade, and the opening to China will shake down and permit common interests in a reordered system to make themselves felt.

The case for greater cooperation and common action among the advanced nations of North America, Western Europe, and Japan has been made frequently on general grounds. The supporting reasons are many and cogent. It is difficult to conceive of a sound world order in the absence of such cooperation. In our analysis of Middle East problems, the argument runs more from the particular to the general. A search for mutually supporting policies in a region outside the direct relations of the advanced industrial nations among themselves, while needing no extraordinary justification, might help in restoring a sense of common purpose none can afford to lose.